Advance Praise for *The Inspired Life*

"An inspired read—from explaining how the brain works, to identifying your greatest obstacles, to describing the ingredients to create an inspired life. Chock-full of powerful 'Inspired Life Action' exercises."
—Dr. Frank Bonkowski, creator of the website Happiness After Midlife

"*The Inspired Life* is a life-map with the potential to change your life and change the world. Susyn and Joan are wise women and skilled master teachers who provide you with the ingredients that generate limitless possibility to expand your capacity to give and receive love. Whether or not you know your inspired life vision or are in the midst of a breakdown, or are wondering what your next step is, using this book offers you the key to the life you desire."
—Mary Angela Buffo, owner and director of
Ananda Yoga & Wellness Center in Southampton, NY

"We all want to live an inspired life, but it can seem so elusive. Susyn Reeve and Joan Breiner have cracked the code. 'Inspiration' sounds like something out there, but it's not. It's something inside—and you and only you can find it. How? *The Inspired Life* has all the tools and support you need to wake up from the trance, make new choices, and upgrade the software of your mind. *The Inspired Life* is truly knowledge in action."
—Janet Conner, author of
Writing Down Your Soul and *My Soul Pages*

"This isn't just another inspiring book. It both insp͟i͟r͟   ͟es you the tools to turn your own life ͟   ͟d others. If you truly want to chan͟   ͟kes, *The Inspired Life* can be your w͟

—Diana Dai͟   *Couples*

- 2013

"*The Inspired Life* brings a refreshingly realistic view of the daily barriers preventing us from engaging in an inspired life. Susyn Reeve and Joan Breiner are handing us the keys to regain control over our thoughts, feelings, emotions, and behaviors. With these keys we can begin to open the doors of commitment, courage, and vision, allowing us to obtain the inspiration from within ourselves. If you are thirsting for a life full of motivation, passion, and celebration where you make the choices and you decide the future, then Reeve and Breiner's *The Inspired Life* is the stepping stone to begin your journey."

—Trevor Moawad, Director of the IMG Performance Institute

"Susyn and Joan have created a delightful book in *The Inspired Life*—straightforward and easy to understand—that will help you get your life on track step-by-step. You will feel nourished and supported along the way—don't miss the opportunity to learn from these amazing women!"

—Dr. Sheri Rosenthal, author of
The Complete Idiot's Guide to Toltec Wisdom

"*The Inspired Life* is a personal growth experience that compels readers to take responsibility for making life happen, rather than letting life happen to them. This book is full of personal stories, wonderful quotes, and practical advice with activities to inspire joyful living. I recommend this book to life coaches and therapists as a guide and a gift to all clients."

—Bob Younglove,
President of the International Council for Self-Esteem

"Inspiration, heartfelt stories, and helpful exercises fill the pages of *The Inspired Life* by Susyn Reeve with Joan Breiner. Open to any page and not only will you unleash your mind's capacity for greater love and joy, you will find mouth-watering nourishment for your inspired life vision."

—Amy Zerner and Monte Farber, authors of
The Soulmate Path and *The Enchanted Birthday Book*

THE
INSPIRED
LIFE

THE
INSPIRED
LIFE

UNLEASHING YOUR MIND'S CAPACITY FOR JOY

SUSYN REEVE WITH JOAN BREINER

EDITIONS

Published in the United States by Viva Editions,
an imprint of Cleis Press, Inc.,
2246 Sixth Street, Berkeley, California 94710.

Printed in the United States.
Cover design: Scott Idleman/Blink
Cover photograph: Meg Takamura/Getty Images
Text design: Frank Wiedemann
First Edition.
10 9 8 7 6 5 4 3 2 1

Trade paper ISBN: 978-1-936740-01-7
E-book ISBN: 978-1-936740-07-9

Permissions appear on page 221.

Library of Congress Cataloging-in-Publication Data

Reeve, Susyn.
 The inspired life : unleashing your mind's capacity for joy / Susyn Reeve
with Joan Breiner. -- 1st ed.
    p. cm.
 ISBN 978-1-936740-01-7 (pbk. : alk. paper)
1. Mind and body. 2. Self-actualization (Psychology) 3. Inspiration. 4.
Positive psychology. I. Breiner, Joan. II. Title.
 BF161.R33 2011
 158.1--dc23
                                        2011026748

*To my grandchildren, Solange and Rhone, you inspire
me to be the best me I can be.*

—Susyn

*To my husband, Bruce, for his support and acceptance
of my desire to continually express myself.*

—Joan

PREFACE
BY KATHERINE WOODWARD THOMAS

To be inspired is to awaken to ourselves as integral parts of something so much larger than our own little lives. It is the quickening of purpose that springs from the depths of our souls. It is the recognition that our brief and precious lives have been given to us so that we might serve to actively midwife our unmanifest potentials for greater levels of goodness, truth, beauty, and love into the manifest world. It is the awakened understanding that we are not here as passive observers of life, or worse yet, as victims of the way things are, but rather, as the very vehicles through which the creative possibilities of what life could be, emerge.

To be inspired, or perhaps we could say, to be in-spirited, means you have offered yourself up to the larger evolutionary process of life itself in order to bring into the world those things that do not yet exist. In understanding that life is actually seeking to get somewhere—call it a transformed world, a harmonious, just, and sustainable human society, or even simply Heaven on Earth—we become aware that life's only way of realizing these things is through you, through me, and through all of us together.

The fastest way to the realization of your own highly inspired life is to ride the wave of that which Great Spirit

(God, Goddess, Higher Power, Spirit, Allah) is already seeking to bring forth into human experience, fully surrendering your life, to be used in service to this great and glorious unfolding. To be so in-spirited is to be joined in full co-creative partnership with the energies of life force itself, listening deeply for your next steps as you follow the gumdrops in the forest to bring forth your most delicious, juicy, dynamic, and creative life of contribution and care.

As there is only one of you in all the universe, the ways that you yourself are called to participate in this great evolutionary process of life are unique to you, and the cost is great should you somehow fail to find your way home to your own creative and in-spirited center. We all know horror stories of those who lived contracted lesser lives and left this world without ever realizing their potentials or fulfilling their dreams. As a matter of fact, we must admit that this is actually the more common experience than that of living a fully inspired life. Perhaps you yourself are in danger of becoming one of those who never rises to the occasion of your life, and this is what has motivated you to pick up this book. If this is so for you, you've done the exact right thing. For so much is at stake in you becoming yourself fully, not just for yourself, but for all of us. For you hold the seeds of gifts and greatness within you that the world has never seen and will never see again after you are gone. It is not only a loss for the one who never blossoms, but also for all of us if your particularly beautiful fragrance never finds its way into our collective garden.

Yet, be heartened, for you are in the right place. What my dear colleagues, Susyn and Joan, have created is nothing short of an in-spirited manual of love, offering a gorgeous step-by-step guide toward the realization of your most inspired and meaningful life. That they do so with deep transparency, authenticity, wisdom, and heart makes them both highly relatable and deeply trustworthy. It's as though you're being granted wisdom in stereo from two loving friends you know beyond a shadow of a doubt are on your side and rooting for you, women who've been around the block a few times and know exactly of which they speak.

In this time of great transformation and turmoil, it is easy to turn away and move toward trying to organize our lives around feeling more safe and secure, dimming ourselves down for fear of getting our heads chopped off. However, what the world truly needs right now are those of us who have the courage to come fully alive, who bravely offer ourselves up with open hearts and open minds to take on living our most fully realized, most highly creative, and most deeply inspired lives.

Katherine Woodward Thomas
Co-founder/co-leader of the Feminine Power Global
Community
www.femininepower.com
April 2011

ACKNOWLEDGMENTS

Any creative project is the result of a community of support. This book has been brought to life through the encouragement and loving support of our family, friends, and the dedicated team at Viva Editions.

Gail Lynne Goodwin (inspiremetoday.com), David Riklan (selfgrowth.com), and Katherine Woodward Thomas (femininepower.com) are true visionaries who readily agreed to being interviewed when the book was no more than an idea. Their belief in this project propelled and inspired us to write a book that weds our passion with practical actions that everyone can use to live their vision of an inspired life.

This book would not have been possible without the Viva Editions Team:

Brenda Knight, Associate Publisher, has midwifed this project from its conception by helping us develop the concept, providing excellent editorial support, and introducing *The Inspired Life* to an audience beyond our wildest imaginings. She is the cheerleader of authors' dreams.

Felice Newman, Publisher extraordinaire, in inviting us to call her or email her at any time with our questions and thoughts, clearly demonstrated that we had the full support of Viva Editions throughout the process of bringing *The Inspired Life* to the marketplace.

Nancy Fish's willingness to generously offer ideas and help us refine ours is a crucial factor in bringing our vision to life and of course to the marketplace! And Kat Sanborn and Kara Wuest, your expertise and support have been invaluable.

Our families—Kevin, Maya, Solange, and Rhone Baker; David Rattiner and all the members of the Kelly, McPherson, and Tyndall families; Bruce Breiner, the Breiner children, and grandchildren; and Joan's mom, Rita Weinstock, who passed on during the writing of this book, have been a constant source of inspiration, and it is through their love and presence in our lives that we are role models for the possibility of living an inspired life.

Our friends—Steve Bankert, Mary Angela Buffo, Johanna Chase, Calla Crafts, Diana Daffner, Eve Eliot, Ann Fragele, Sheryl Hastalis, Lynn Neidorf, Judith Noel, Susan Robinson, Lorraine Simone, Joanne Thompson, Ilonka Tumelaire, Jane Umanoff—are priceless treasures in our lives. Their willingness to be interviewed (even when we weren't sure if their words would make it into the book) or discuss the book and their curiosity about our progress kept us on track. A special thanks to our dear, beautiful friend, Melinda Lee, whose life is a daily reflection of what it means to embody your dreams.

Our clients are a constant source of inspiration for

us. Their courage and commitment to live inspired lives is a daily testament that the possibility of fulfillment and joy is the birthright of all people. Their willingness to use breakdowns as breakthroughs is a potent reminder of the elasticity and power of the human spirit.

Katherine Woodward Thomas your willingness to find time in your much much too busy schedule to write the Preface is a priceless gift. You are truly an Angel, capturing the message of this book so beautifully. Your presence is an inspiration in our lives.

And a special thank you to the public libraries in Lee, MA, Sarasota, FL, Venice, FL, East Hampton, NY, and Hampton Bays, NY. You provided quiet sanctuaries that invited our ideas to easily flow through our fingertips onto our computer screens.

Finally, we deeply acknowledge one another—our friendship is a constant source of love, inspiration, and support, for more than thirty years. Our personal and professional lives have thrived in the presence of one another.

PART ONE:
INTRODUCTION

HOW TO USE THIS BOOK

We wrote this book to inspire you to cultivate, nurture, and live your vision of an inspired life. Our intention is to illuminate the path, to unleash the power of your mind to the vast creative potential and possibility alive in each one of us. We will guide you to identify and acknowledge your uninspired thinking and support you to move through your resistance by providing concepts, stories, and exercises to cultivate the inspired life of your dreams.

In Part One, we introduce how to use this book and extend our invitation to live your vision of an inspired life. We share stories of our personal journeys and encourage you to make the choice to join us.

In Part Two, we provide information about how the brain works and the creative process. Scientific research has demonstrated that you have the ability to upgrade the software of your mind and create brain pathways that allow for habits of thought to generate emotions and actions supporting the life you desire.

In Part Three, we guide you in identifying and acknowledging your internal resistance—your uninspired thinking which, when accepted as truth, is your greatest obstacle to living an inspired life.

In Part Four, we elaborate the ingredients necessary to create and sustain an inspired life. We provide the concepts, illuminated through inspiring quotes and stories combined with practices, exercises, and power statements to embody the ideas in your life. Keep in mind that while understanding what the ingredients of an inspired life are, putting them into practice—walking the talk—is the essential key to living your vision of your inspired life.

Some of the concepts will resonate and feel right on target for you while others will challenge your way of thinking. For this reason, we encourage you to suspend your judgment knowing that transforming your life requires that you change your habits of thought and behavior—and this is not always comfortable.

THERE ARE MANY WAYS TO WORK WITH THIS BOOK:

- ❀ Read and complete each chapter in sequential order.

- ❀ Skim the table of contents and focus on what "calls" to you.

- ❀ Open the book and read and complete the inspired life action for that chapter, although we do suggest that you read How the Brain Works (page 29) and The Power of Thoughts

4

(page 32) to provide a framework to understand how you transform uninspired thinking to inspired thinking.

❀ Form an inspired life group—face-to-face or via a conference call—and discuss each chapter, your experience with practicing the exercises, and your successes. (See the Appendix for specific instructions to form an inspired life circle, page 207.)

Be patient and compassionate with yourself as you become familiar with this information and put it into practice in your life. Read the chapters and follow the inspired life actions *at your own pace*. These activities are designed to guide you in applying the concepts in your daily life and serve as a springboard for upgrading the software of your mind and evolving your thoughts and behaviors—for transforming your life.

WE APPLAUD AND CELEBRATE YOUR GREATNESS, IN WHICH:

❀ You are connected to an infinite source of loving energy.

❀ You are whole and empowered in the present moment.

❀ You experience life as a source of infinite creative possibility.

❀ You use breakdowns as opportunities to break through limiting patterns of the past.

❀ You appreciate and value yourself, generously sharing your gifts, talents, and abilities with your family, friends, coworkers, community, and the larger global community.

OUR INVITATION TO YOU

It was the best of times, it was the worst of times, it was the age of wisdom, it was the age of foolishness, it was the epoch of belief, it was the epoch of incredulity, it was the season of Light, it was the season of Darkness, it was the spring of hope, it was the winter of despair, we had everything before us, we had nothing before us, we were all going direct to heaven, we were all going direct the other way—in short, the period was so far like the present period, that some of its noisiest authorities insisted on its being received, for good or for evil, in the superlative degree of comparison only.

—Charles Dickens, A Tale of Two Cities

There have been many names for and descriptions of the times we are living in. Some consider this to be a New Age, others the Age of Aquarius. To some it is the End Times with doomsday quickly approaching. Some believe the end of the Mayan calendar is simply an astronomical occurrence while others define it as the end of civilization as we know it; still others say while it marks an end, it is a gateway to a new beginning of peace and cooperation among all peoples.

Charles Dickens's words from his classic novel continue to ring true today.

The worst of times: When watching and listening to news reports it becomes clear that there is currently much strife and cruelty in the world: war, genocide, ethnic cleansing, the stoning of women, which always amazes me since the ones hurling the stones were birthed through the bodies of women—their mothers. Economic conditions throughout the world are worse than they have been in decades. The divide between the rich and the poor widens daily as the middle class disappears. Children are starving throughout the world while the military budgets of nations get larger and larger. In the United States partisan politics is so focused on who is "right" and who is "wrong" that it seems that issues—even the role and purpose of government itself—get lost in the desire to win elections. Corporate greed and government scandals fill the airwaves and leaders are not trusted. News pundits weave stories of fear and terror as their nightly offering. Natural disasters seem to be rapidly increasing. Is the current recurrence of bedbugs a plague in our midst? Hate crimes based on gender, race, ethnicity, sexual orientation abound. Not only is there hatred among racial and ethnic groups throughout the world, families can't even get along.

The best of times: Since the first photograph, the famous

"Blue Marble," in which Earth is in full view was taken on December 7, 1972, as the *Apollo 17* crew left Earth's orbit, there is no doubt that we are One—one humanity on one planet. Since that time, our inter-connectedness and inter-dependence has been made more and more evident through the Internet via Twitter, Facebook, and blogs, which offer instant access to social networks and world-wide communities (and playing a significant role in the call for democracy in the Middle East); the global economy and the resources and support that are readily offered, not only by governments, but also by people throughout the world within hours of reports of disasters. Advances in research have provided life-saving procedures and reme-dies. Educational opportunities abound. There is a global movement afoot honoring Mother Earth, our true home. Green industries are becoming mainstream. At the same time the evolution of consciousness continues with more and more people committing to live Gandhi's words, *"Be the change you wish to see in the world."* Individuals and groups are reaching across borders and boundaries in the name of peace. Women throughout the world are stepping forward committed to peace and our voices are growing and the fruits of these labors are being felt.

Katherine Woodward Thomas and Claire Zammit lead "Calling in the One" and "Feminine Power Mastery" tele-classes with thousands of participants representing more than fifty countries worldwide. In these programs, women and men in a community of support declare their commitment to live their inspired life visions, to be love made manifest in their relationships with themselves, their families, and their local and global communities.

Whatever you may believe, isn't now the time to enrich your life by affirming and committing to your inspired life vision? At the very least, living your vision offers you the possibility of greater joy, fulfillment, and happiness. And, at best, as you put your stake in the ground for living a more peaceful and loving life, your consciousness generating your actions contributes to the collective consciousness of the Greater Field of Life, and love grows and peace expands for all.

In 2001 the Hopi Elders said, in a message that continues to be relevant today:

WE ARE THE ONES WE'VE BEEN WAITING FOR

You have been telling the people that this is the Eleventh Hour. Now you must go back and tell the people that this is The Hour. And there are things to be considered:

- ❀ Where are you living?
- ❀ What are you doing?
- ❀ What are your relationships?
- ❀ Are you in right relation?
- ❀ Where is your water?
- ❀ Know your garden.
- ❀ It is time to speak your Truth.
- ❀ Create your community.
- ❀ Be good to each other.
- ❀ And do not look outside yourself for the leader.

This could be a good time!

There is a river flowing now very fast. It is so great and swift that there are those who will be afraid. They will try to hold on to the shore. They will feel they are being torn apart, and they will suffer greatly.

Know the river has its destination. The elders say we must let go of the shore, push off into the middle of the

11

river, keep our eyes open and our heads above the water. See who is in there with you and celebrate.

At this time in history, we are to take nothing personally. Least of all, ourselves. For the moment that we do, our spiritual growth and journey comes to a halt.

The time of the lone wolf is over. Gather yourselves! Banish the word struggle *from your attitude and your vocabulary.*

All that we do now must be done in a sacred manner and in celebration.

We are the ones we've been waiting for.

Now is the time, because now is the time you are alive. Now is the time you have this precious gift of life on Earth. Now is the time, as you declare and embody your inspired life vision that you open the door to Heaven on Earth.

This book is our invitation to you to join us.

With love and faith in your vision,
Susyn & Joan

OUR INSPIRED LIFE JOURNEYS: OUR STORIES

An Inspired Life is one in which I allow all the ebbs and flows of life to feed me and move me forward.

—Jody Florman

Susyn

For as long as I can remember, I have felt a deep longing to be happy, to experience joy, which was my way of saying I wanted to live an inspired life. Yes, I have many happy memories and I have been told repeatedly that my unconventional life has been an inspiration for others to articulate and follow their dreams. But for a very long time joy and happiness appeared as a distant hope that I was always reaching for yet never quite grabbing hold of. There were moments of happiness—and some of them lasted for quite a while, for years, but the foundation was wobbly until I accepted that my relationship with myself was the primary determinant of living an inspired life.

I was a wanted and loved child. I have no story of abuse and lack of care but that didn't stop me from believing that I wasn't loved as a result of my mom's hospitalization for about ten days, when I was three years old, and my parents decided it best for me to stay with my grandparents. I didn't last there for ten days but in the five days I was there I subconsciously made meaning of my circumstances that would plague me for decades to come. My mom and I had many conversations when I was in my thirties, forties, and fifties in which she described how a different child returned home after that time with my grandparents. The happy, carefree, giggling child I had been was replaced by a sullen, withdrawn little girl who had moments of breaking out of this armor but quickly returned to that default position.

I had never spent a day away from my family before this and the trauma of this separation left me feeling abandoned and unloved. The beliefs that nourished these feelings: they don't love me, I'm bad and no matter what I do I will never really be loved, imprisoned me much of my life. It is these beliefs, my particular version of I'm not enough, which were my major obstacles to living an inspired life.

You may think that it is the circumstances of your life that are the cause of your misery and suffering. While life's challenges can certainly take the wind out of your sails and rob you of your passion, faith, trust, and belief in possibility and in yourself, it is your relationship with yourself and the meaning that you give to the circumstances of your *life that are the potent blocks to living an inspired life.*

Programmed with the belief that I wasn't loved—as though it was hardwired into my brain—I began to see the world and accumulate evidence for the validity of this belief. And, let me tell you, it was not difficult to see evidence since my beliefs informed the meaning I attributed to all the circumstances of my life. As a teen I was so certain that I wasn't loved that I was very shy around boys; I didn't know what to say to them, so I often wasn't chosen by them. Proof that I wasn't loved was right before my eyes, my girlfriends had boyfriends, but I didn't. So I decided I would be the smart one, my older sister taking the prized position of the pretty one in my family. I was so certain that I was unloved that when I was sixteen years old I systematically eliminated the word love *from my vocabulary.*

I have a clear memory of being with a friend, listening to the Beatles on our transistor radios and saying, "I love this song," and then quickly correcting myself by saying aloud, "I don't mean I love the song, I mean I like it." For years I did not use the word love, *and then used it only after much consideration. When I look back on this now, it is clear that here was a powerful example of our ability to choose our thoughts and directly influence our experience...but at the time I was years away from taking responsibility for my part as the artist of my life—the co-creator of my experience with my thoughts as a primary tool in my artist toolbox.*

Decades of my life I searched to find the key, the answer, that would, ZAP, lead me to the end of my journey and joy would be mine forevermore and, of course, I would be loved. At first, I was hyper-vigilant seeing how others reacted to me as the indicator of whether or not I was loved. If I was asked out on a date, I was loved; if he didn't call again, I wasn't. If my mother criticized my wildly curly hair I was unloved—and the truth is that until I was in my early fifties I heard most of what my mom said as criticism.

I became a self-help addict. Starting with therapy when I was seventeen years old, then getting a Master's Degree in Counseling, then one workshop after another, Silva Mind Control, est, DMA (Dimensional Macrostructural Alignment or Doesn't Mean Anything!), a month at Esalen, Landmark Education, Twelve Step programs, workshops with Joseph Campbell, Jean Houston, Mary Manin Morrissey, don Miguel Ruiz, Katherine Woodward Thomas, interspersed with gestalt therapy, NLP (Neuro-linguistic Programming), energy work, group therapy, yoga, bodywork, sprinkled with marijuana, LSD, magic mushrooms, ecstasy, ayahuasca. I became a counselor, a coach, a minister—and thousands of people invited me to be their guide on their journey to live an inspired life, to be happy, to feel loved. I became familiar with our inner landscape, and was able to navigate very dark places with my clients giving them the encouragement and the tools to see and reach the light at the end of the tunnel.

Initially I looked outside of myself for the missing pieces of the puzzle, hoping that this workshop or that teacher would provide the answer, the relief from my ongoing misery. I changed the circumstances of my life—moved, was sexually promiscuous, married, raised stepchildren, traveled, divorced, was celibate, wrote books, met fascinating people, followed my heart's desire, took risks and along the way discovered the elements of an inspired life. What I know for sure is that it has been easier for me to identify what these elements are than it has been to actually commit to taking responsibility for applying them in my life. But knowledge without action, at best, leads only to momentary satisfaction.

I learned that to upgrade the software of my mind, to create new brain pathways, and to cultivate new habits of thought and behavior to live an inspired life requires:

❀ *an understanding of the creative process— what it is, how it works, and my part in it,*

❀ *a clear vision to serve as a beacon, a guide- post, my north star,*

❀ *the courageous choice to acknowledge and transform all the beliefs that are at odds with my vision,*

❀ *taking responsibility for the thoughts I think, the words I speak, and the actions I take,*

❀ *a connection with Source Energy, God, the Greater Field of Life as my co-creative partner.*

It has now been many years that I have consciously lived an inspired life. I actually believed about ten years ago that I had this handled. Life was good. I knew the formula, and I was following it. But life is an ever-evolving process, and as recently as this morning, I questioned if I have it in me to complete this book, to exercise regularly, to be at peace with food, to have the relationship of my dreams. So, what did I do? I reminded myself of my vision of unprecedented love in my life and that my capacity to give and receive love is forever evolving—deepening and expanding, and that breakdowns are doorways to breakthroughs. And even though summer had overnight become a cold, windy, gray day I put on my sneakers and went out for my exercise walk, I chose food to eat that tastes delicious and is nutritious, I sat down and wrote, and when I looked in the mirror I bellowed, "I love you," since loving myself is a necessary condition for living my inspired life vision.

Joan

Until I was about five years old, my life was fun, happy, and all-around great. Being the first girl born into an upwardly mobile family I was showered with attention and told I was adorable. I did not experience worry, anxiety, and inadequacy. But right after my fifth birthday party, life as I knew it changed. Starting with the death of my great grandmother, suddenly this very important person in my life was no longer present to shower me with unconditional love.

School started and I immediately discovered that I was different than the other kids. I was taller, I had red hair, and my face was polka-dotted with big freckles. In addition, due to my learning disabilities, I was definitely not as smart as the other kids in my class. These issues plagued me throughout all of my school years.

Kids made fun of me and often brought me to tears. I had very few friends and I was definitely not part of the "in" crowd. Due to my learning disability I needed tutoring and extra help. There was also no denying that at six-foot-one I was taller than most. I felt miserable and inadequate. These feelings continued through my twenties. But, when I was thirty years old, I decided that enough was enough and I got my first taste of what it is to live an inspired life. I took responsibility for my life, instead of waiting around and hoping things were going to get better. I created a vision for myself—grounded in my desire to be happy and experience joy.

When one gets clear and takes responsibility things have an amazing, seemingly magical way of falling into place. I met Susyn Reeve, my dear friend and coauthor of this book. She introduced me to focused concentration, a form of meditation.

Meditation was my key for feeling better about myself. When I meditated I felt at peace, detached from what had been the voice of constant criticism in my mind, and this peace of mind and well-being extended far beyond the time I sat with my eyes closed and my attention focused on my breath. I felt empowered and hopeful. My thoughts and feelings about myself changed. I started to live in possibility as opposed to misery.

Living in possibility led me to study ways to nourish happiness in my life. I discovered that there are many things I could do to change the way I felt and operated in the world. I have learned that an inspired life can be cultivated and when it is life is full of synchronicities and joy.

Now, at age sixty-two, I still have a learning disability, I am still tall, and my hair is now artificially red. The same issues that were present when I was five years old are still present, but I am in control of how I feel and I feel good! I am proud of who I am and what I have accomplished in my life. I have created miracles for myself. I have created and sold a successful business. I am married for twenty-

seven years to a loving man. I own a beautiful home on the water in Sarasota, FL, and I am helping people get in touch with their greatness.

This book is about sharing the information and techniques which have worked for me and others, so you, too, can live your vision of an inspired life.

MAKE THE CHOICE

Life is a sum of all your choices.

—Albert Camus

Are you ready to live an inspired life rooted in the sacred union of your body-mind-spirit, grounded in your vision, and reflected in your thoughts, words, and actions? It all begins with making a choice, with saying, *"Yes, I choose to live an inspired life."*

This is an empowering choice. So, heed this cautionary note: When you make this choice, it is possible, actually most likely, that in addition to experiencing greater joy, happiness, peace, and self-worth, you will initially encounter distress, frustration, turmoil, emotional pain, sadness, and anxiety. This is natural and normal. It is the process of your personal blocks and obstacles to living an inspired life—your internal resistance—coming to the surface of your conscious awareness, presenting you with the choice to evolve beyond these patterns of the past.

When your fears and beliefs—*I'm not good enough, I'm unworthy, I'm not loved, I'm powerless, etc.*—meet the light of your awareness you then have the opportunity to acknowledge them and use them as a springboard to upgrade the software of your mind, transforming your identity to *I am worthy, I am loving, I am valuable, I am loveable, etc...*

It is as if by choosing to live an inspired life you are making the choice to clean house, after not having cleaned for many years. This choice means you will be relying on your vision, inner strength, trust, and faith to make decisions and act on them, regardless of your internal resistance as you transform your beliefs and your relationship with yourself.

Living an inspired life requires that you exercise discipline and make conscious choices regarding your thoughts, beliefs, emotions, words, and actions. The more you do this, the more successful you will be. Conscious inspired thinking is a learned skill that demands practice to gain proficiency, giving way to joyfully living an inspired life.

Know that if you have already lived with the pain of low self-esteem, lack of confidence, anxiety, and fear then you are capable of moving through the distress of this transformative process to create new patterns of thought— new brain pathways—which will naturally result in your living the life you desire. How do we know this is possible? Because we have done it and we have helped thousands of people make this choice and reap the rewards of living their vision of an inspired life.

An inspired life is right in front of each and every one of us...embrace it and it is yours. Every moment is a blessing.

—Gil Williams

So, if you are ready for the most glorious adventure of your life, start now by following the directions below and formally making the conscious choice to live an Inspired Life:

1. Make yourself comfortable, preferably sitting in front of a mirror, with your spine straight, your feet flat on the floor, your hands resting on your thighs, and your eyes closed.

2. Concentrate on your breath. The way it flows in and out, like a tide. Flowing in through your nose and out through your mouth. Follow the path of your breath as it circulates through your body from the top of your head down through to the bottom of your feet.

3. Take five full, deep inhalations and exhalations.

4. Open your eyes, look in the mirror, and say aloud (allowed): *"I Choose an Inspired Life. I*

Choose to Live an Inspired Life. I Am Living an Inspired Life."

If ever you feel scared or alone, take the inspired life action of asking for help. Talk to a trusted family member or friend who will witness and love you and not fuel the flames of your fears and worries. Meet with a counselor or coach.

Remember: Opening this book, starting to read it and putting into action the information within it, is a powerful reflection of your commitment to co-creating and living an inspired life. You are on your way.

PART TWO:
YOUR BRAIN
AND YOUR THOUGHTS

HOW THE BRAIN WORKS

A mind once stretched by a new idea, never regains its original dimension.

—Oliver Wendell Holmes, Jr.

Since living an inspired life has its roots in your mind, it is necessary to understand how your mind works, how new brain pathways are created, and how upgraded software of the mind is installed.

Dr. Bruce Lipton, in his book *The Biology of Belief*, describes his groundbreaking work in the field of New Biology providing powerful scientific information about how the brain works based on cell biology. Dr. Lipton is a former medical school professor and research scientist. His experiments, and those of other leading-edge scientists, have examined in great detail the processes by which cells receive information. The implications of this research radically change our understanding of life. It shows that genes and DNA do not control our biology; instead, DNA is controlled by signals from outside the cell, including the energetic messages emanating from our positive and negative thoughts. Dr. Lipton's profoundly hopeful synthesis of the latest and best research in cell biology and quantum physics is being hailed as a major breakthrough showing that our bodies and our experience can be changed as we retrain our thinking.

Your mind is constantly changing. Every time you have a new thought, a new neuro-pathway is formed in your brain—a new train of thought. To live an inspired life your mind must cultivate empowering thoughts through your beliefs, assumptions, agreements, words, feelings, choices, and actions.

As a single footstep will not make a path on the earth, so a single thought will not make a pathway in the mind. To make a deep physical path, we walk again and again. To make a deep mental path, we must think over and over the kind of thoughts we wish to dominate our lives.

—Henry David Thoreau

Here is how it works: The brain is made up of cells called neurons. These cells have nerve endings called synapses and dendrites. Nerve endings release chemical and electrical stimuli to communicate with each other. This communication forms neural-pathways in the brain and is the basis for how the brain works. For every thought you have, there is corresponding communication between the neurons in your brain.

When you initially learn something, the pathway

is weak. Neuro-pathways that are habitually used (consciously or unconsciously) are the "path well traveled." It is easy for your mind to follow these pathways, these routes, and they become your dominant and automatic thoughts and beliefs, which then generate your feelings—your energetic frequency.

Think about when you first learned to ride a bike. You had to consciously pay attention to staying balanced, keeping your eyes on the road, holding onto the handlebars, and steering in your desired direction. In addition, your feelings probably included feeling scared, unsure, and frustrated. Then, the more you practiced the stronger your bicycle-riding brain pathways became and your feelings of confidence and certainty in your bicycle-riding expertise flourished.

Eventually, you were able to get on your bike and ride without thinking. You were operating on automatic. A strong brain pathway had been created as though a new brain software application had been uploaded and was seamlessly operating in your mind.

THE POWER OF THOUGHTS

All that we are is the result of what we have thought.

The mind is everything. What we think we become.

—Siddhartha Gautama Buddha

Your mind works the same way in how you think about yourself, others, and life. As a child your thoughts about yourself and the world were formed from the messages you heard, interpreted, and believed from the important and influential people in your life.

For example, if you were continually made fun of by classmates and not invited to play with them when you were a child, you have probably developed low self-esteem and disempowered thought patterns regarding friends and social situations. As a result, as an adult, obsessive thinking reflecting these patterns may automatically surface in social gatherings where you experience anxiety, fear, and nervousness based on thoughts like:

❀ People don't like me.

❀ I was only invited because they had to invite me.

❀ Nobody's going to talk to me.

❀ I don't know what to say.

An inspired mind knows these thoughts are simply thoughts, and, although they may be dominant, they *can be changed*! Creating new neuro-pathway connections, patterns, and habits requires:

❀ an embodied vision and intention,

❀ desire reflected in your feelings and emotional energy,

❀ committing to a conscious choice,

❀ taking action (consistent practice), like learning to ride a bike,

❀ acknowledging and celebrating the journey.

The challenge you face in creating new brain pathways is that as humans we are used to operating on automatic and are most often asleep to the thoughts we are thinking. Just as the majority of us are asleep to the software programs that operate our electronic gadgets! (I have to admit, I love my iPhone, Kindle reader, Flip camera, and new Mac computer—and I don't even want to know any details about their software—I just want them to work easily.)

How do you wake up and become aware of the thoughts that form your beliefs, about how you feel about yourself given that you think thousands of thoughts each and every day? And how do you create new brain pathways to nurture and nourish your vision of an inspired life?

The answer is: You identify your current dominant thoughts and makeup, *yes*, then create new thoughts that support the inspired life you desire! This awareness combined with commitment to action and consistent focus allows you to upgrade and install new patterns of thinking.

Use the following lists as a starting point to identify the dominant thoughts that you are ready and willing to transform and the new thoughts you choose to think.

- ❀ I am unworthy.
- ❀ I am inadequate.
- ❀ I am a failure.
- ❀ I am angry.
- ❀ I am stupid.
- ❀ I am guilty.
- ❀ I can't succeed.
- ❀ I can't get what I want.
- ❀ I will never be loved.
- ❀ I am cursed.
- ❀ I am helpless.
- ❀ I hate myself.
- ❀ I am not a good person.
- ❀ There is something wrong with me.
- ❀ People cannot be trusted.
- ❀ I cannot control my thoughts.
- ❀ I lack confidence.
- ❀ I never get it right.
- ❀ Nothing works for me.
- ❀ I can't count on anyone.
- ❀ Nobody understands me.
- ❀ I don't deserve happiness.
- ❀ Other: (fill in your own thought not listed).

- ❀ I am worthy.
- ❀ I am capable.
- ❀ I am patient.
- ❀ I am smart.
- ❀ I am generous.
- ❀ I am accepting of myself.
- ❀ I am successful.
- ❀ I acknowledge my accomplishments.
- ❀ I am a co-creative partner with the Greater Field of Life.
- ❀ I generously express my love.
- ❀ I am loved.
- ❀ I love and like myself.
- ❀ I am a good person.
- ❀ I am trustworthy.
- ❀ I consciously choose my thoughts.
- ❀ I am confident.
- ❀ I value and appreciate my talents, skills, and abilities.
- ❀ I ask for and allow help and support.
- ❀ I have close, satisfying relationships.
- ❀ I am happy.
- ❀ I am creative.
- ❀ Every day I deepen and expand my capacity to receive and give love.

❀ I live an inspired life.

❀ Other: (fill in your own thought not listed).

An inspired life comes with thinking good thoughts. To think good thoughts, however, requires effort. So train your mind to dwell on sweet perfumes, the touch of silk, tender raindrops against the window, the curve of a flower arrangement, the tranquility of dawn. Then at length, you won't have to make such a great effort and you will be of value to yourself, a value to your profession, and bring honor to the world.

—Lynn Neidorf, after James Clavell

INSPIRED LIFE EXERCISE:

TRANSFORM UNINSPIRED THOUGHTS

Use this exercise to identify dominant thoughts you want to transform and the new thoughts you want to think. Using the lists on pages pages 35–36, circle the Uninspired Life Thoughts that have been dominant in your life that you are ready to transform and the new Inspired Life Thoughts you are ready to install in your mind to create inspired life brain pathways. Whenever you notice an Uninspired Life Thought capturing your attention, acknowledge yourself for noticing and then refocus your attention on the new software—an Inspired Life Thought.

Susyn used this practice during her separation and divorce. Here's her experience:

During my separation and divorce I was constantly imagining how happy my former husband and his new girlfriend were. Each time I focused on their happiness I was convinced that I wasn't pretty, that no man would ever love me and that I would be unhappy forever. These thoughts dominated my thinking and were particularly evident when I drove past the house I had lived in with him that he now shared with his girlfriend.

Every time I drove down that street, the thoughts began: "I bet they're happy all the time. I'm fat and ugly and no one is ever going to love me again." I thought these thoughts on automatic and with great conviction.

Then one day it occurred to me that there was no reason to keep driving down that street and gazing at my old house. There was also no reason to torture myself with painful thoughts. So I made a list of things I could think about that were satisfying to me. Things like the twinkling of the sun dancing on the water when I walked my dog on the beach, my favorite ice cream, spending time with my friends, and my delightful grandchildren. Of course, I could always focus my attention on my breath.

I then made a commitment to myself that I would not drive down that street, and whenever I noticed that I was focusing my attention on thoughts about my former husband and his girlfriend I would turn my attention to a good feeling thought.

I have to admit that it did take a lot of energy, effort and many, many months for me to transform my thinking—but I did, bit by bit and day by day. Then came the day when I realized that a few days had gone by and I hadn't thought about them or berated myself at all. I had created a new brain pathway.

Remember: The very act of *noticing* your uninspired thoughts creates the opportunity to form a new brain pathway.

> *Keep your thoughts positive because your thoughts become your words. Keep your words positive because your words become your behaviors. Keep your behaviors positive because your behaviors become your habits. Keep your habits positive because your habits become your values. Keep your values positive because your values become your destiny.*
>
> *—Gandhi*

To guarantee that a new thought will eventually become your dominant brain pathway you must keep in mind that a new thought is not enough on its own, you must embody it. You have to have a somatic experience of your good feeling thought and to actually feel the feelings this new thought evokes to realize the potent benefit of inspired thinking.

Have you ever noticed that when you commit to generating positive thoughts you still hear the voice of doubt, fear, and uncertainty running like an endless recording in your mind? You boldly create an affirmation, *"I focus my attention on positive thoughts, words, and actions."* You commit to writing this affirmation in your journal ten times each morning for the next thirty days to keep focused on your positive intention. You paste sticky notes in strategic locations—your bathroom mirror, your refrigerator door—you write your affirmation on your screen saver, etc... But, whenever you write it and see it you also hear other—negative—affirmations in your mind: *"Who are you kidding? You're so judgmental. This is too hard, what's positive about having more bills than I can pay? I just don't know how to do this."*

Overlaying a positive thought on a belief that is at odds with the affirmation is not enough to upgrade the software of your mind. It's like putting a bandage on a wound without first cleaning the wound and applying the appropriate antiseptic. You won't see the wound directly, but that doesn't mean it doesn't exist. To truly create a new brain pathway based on your inspired thinking, you must free your heart and mind from your uninspired programming, not merely cover it up with a new thought that you really don't believe and are unable to embody.

Remember: While positive thinking is useful for an attitude adjustment, the true source of empowerment resides in you experiencing your inspired thoughts alive in your body in the present moment.

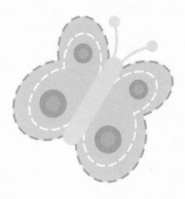

USE YOUR FEELINGS AS YOUR GUIDE

It can be a challenge to pay attention to all your uninspired thoughts, particularly since they have often been given free rein for many years or even decades. When you notice you are feeling unhappy, sad, angry, scared, fearful, hopeless, etc., this is a sign that you are thinking uninspired thoughts. Use these feelings as your guide to discover your dominant thoughts and beliefs by completing this statement: When I am feeling _____, I am thinking/believing _____. You may have more than one belief attached to your feelings so approach this as a detective and uncover as many thoughts as possible that have generated your feelings.

RENEWING AND NOURISHING YOUR BRAIN

*Happiness is always within you. Your thoughts
and feelings hide it, as the clouds hide the sun.
Your mind is your instrument. Learn to be its master and not be its slave.*

—Remez Sasson

An inspired life requires time to renew and go inward.
Spiritual teachers throughout the ages have said that the
Kingdom of Heaven is within. The inner experience of
peace, contentment, and inspiration is considered to be
heaven on earth. Connecting with your personal experience of heaven on earth opens the door to transforming
your relationship in all aspects of your life including:

- ❀ Health—physical, emotional, and spiritual
- ❀ Self-Esteem
- ❀ Personal Relationships
- ❀ Creativity
- ❀ Finances
- ❀ Career
- ❀ Spirituality
- ❀ Fun and Enjoyment

The most potent way of connecting, renewing, and nourishing your experience of heaven on earth is through meditation. Scientific research has shown that when people meditate the workings of their brains—their actual brain chemistry—changes, with powerful short- and long-term consequences. Specifically, the left prefrontal cortex, the region of the brain associated with happiness, positive thoughts, and emotions, is activated. The more you meditate the more you enhance this area of your brain, nourishing peace of mind and well-being as you strengthen the brain pathways that are essential for living an inspired life.

Developing a meditation practice initially requires, in addition to your commitment and patience, a consistent practice in the presence of self-talk, that incessant inner critic that complains, judges, and is used to being in the driver's seat of your mind.

While there are many methods of meditation, all types involve directing your attention on a focal point. Your focal point may be: your breath, a mantra (a word or phrase repeated over and over again), a chant, an object (a candle flame, a flower, a beautiful picture), or a relaxing mental image.

The object is to focus your attention—concentrating on your focal point—to the exclusion of all other thoughts. When you find yourself thinking about something else, like what you have to do when you finish meditating, or wondering how much longer you have to sit still, you simply notice it, accept it, and consciously return your attention to your focal point. Your intent is to learn to control and direct your thoughts, to be the master of your mind.

When Joan discovered the power of meditation her life changed. Here is her story:

Being dyslexic and the tallest girl in my class—I was six-foot-one by the time I was in high school—I struggled with low self-esteem and depression from the early age of five through my early thirties. I felt like life was never going to work out for me. No matter how hard I tried I never seemed to find the right guy, make the right friends, get the right job, or look attractive.

I went to countless hours of therapy, read self-help books, attended personal development workshops and although intellectually I could grasp the concepts, I still continued to struggle with feelings of inadequacy and depression.

When I was thirty-three years old, my friend Susyn introduced me to a course, developed by Robert Fritz, the author of The Path of Least Resistance, *which directed me to suspend my judgments about whether the course was going to work or not. I was encouraged, by Susyn, and by the support of our group, to simply follow the instructions and do the exercises and activities for six weeks and then evaluate whether or not the course had value for me. I agreed.*

Following the course instructions, I listened to audio recordings for ten to twenty minutes every morning and evening. The audio messages directed me to use my mind to focus on parts of my body, my breath, my desires, and my inner guidance. To my amazement, in just six weeks my emotional state completely changed. I became joyful and happy and, as a result, the rest of my life shifted. All of a sudden, as if by magic, things I had wanted my whole life were happening. I attribute it to the meditation techniques that I learned and consistently used. They were and still are, twenty-nine years later, a magical elixir to my psyche.

Now whenever I am feeling uninspired, off-center, and generally not thrilled with life—I go back to the basics. I follow an inspired life action and wake up early in the morning and take fifteen to twenty minutes to tap into the power of my mind by focusing my attention through meditation.

The results are amazing and knowing the physiology of how my brain changes when I meditate makes it even easier for me to meditate. I know when I meditate I am practicing self-care, which translates into self-love and feelings of happiness—into living an inspired life.

INSPIRED LIFE PRACTICE: MEDITATE

Take time to renew and nourish your brain. Make a commitment to meditate three or four times this week and next and notice the impact this has on the quality of your life.

The best time to meditate is in the morning before you begin your day or at the end of the day, but not right before you go to bed when you might immediately fall asleep! Make it a specific time each day, formally creating a meditation practice routine. Initially, meditate for just a few minutes and slowly add more time to your practice. Eventually, meditate for fifteen to twenty minutes.

It helps to pick a specific room or area in your house for your meditation practice. I do not recommend meditating in the room where you work. Using the same room every time you meditate makes it easier for you to get into a meditative state since you associate that place with the experience of peace, contentment, and serenity. Pick a place where you will be free of interruptions. Barbara, one of our coaching clients, brought a pillow to sit on and a candle into the bathroom since that was the only room where she was free from being interrupted by her family! It is okay to have background sounds, such as birds singing, as long as it is relaxing and not distracting and it's a good idea to turn your phone ringtone off.

It is natural to wonder whether you are doing it right. There is no right way. Each time you meditate you will have a different experience. The most important point in meditation is to refocus your attention, free of judgment and criticism, on your focal point as soon as you notice you are thinking about something else and your mind is wandering. The goal of meditation is to let go of your attachment to your outside reality and to cultivate your connection with your inner self. It is OK to glance at a clock to time the meditation, or if you use an alarm, choose a sound that is soft and not jarring.

Use the following meditation instructions or any other meditation practice that has worked for you in the past.

Start by writing down all the things that are cluttering your mind right now, including chores to complete and concerns and questions on your mind. As you write each item down, know that you are clearing your mind to be more fully present in the here and now. When your list is completed, put it down and then:

1. Sit comfortably, with your spine straight, feet flat on the floor, palms resting gently on your thighs, and close your eyes.

2. Take long, slow deep breaths in, breathing right down into your belly and then slowly exhale. Focusing your attention on your breath—inhale a sense of calm and relaxation through your nose and exhale stress and worry completely through your mouth.

3. If you are new to meditation, initially do this for twenty complete inhalations and exhalations, building your practice so that you are focusing on your breath for fifteen to twenty minutes.

Remember: Meditation is a skill; allow yourself time—free of judgment—to develop your practice of mindfulness so that eventually, you approach *all* of life as your practice—focused and alert in the present moment.

WALKING MEDITATION

If you find it challenging to sit and meditate, experiment with a walking meditation:

1. Choose an amount of time for this practice, starting with a couple of minutes and expanding your practice to at least fifteen to twenty minutes.

2. Align your thoughts and actions. Think right as you step forward on your right foot; think left as you step forward on your left foot.

3. As soon as you notice that your thoughts and actions are out of step—out of alignment—make the correction. You may be surprised by the frequency of disconnection between your thoughts and actions.

PART THREE:
WHAT SABOTAGES
AN INSPIRED LIFE

REFRAMING WHAT SABOTAGES AN INSPIRED LIFE

An uninspired life is like a prison—each bar cemented into a foundation of "I can't. I'm afraid, nothing works for me. I'm not enough." The key to unlocking this prison resides in your mind—the thoughts you think, the assumptions you make, and the beliefs that direct your words and actions. Change your thoughts and you change your life. Possibility begins in your mind.

When I think of an uninspired life, the movie, *Groundhog Day*, comes to mind: Phil Connors is the arrogant and egotistical weatherman for local station WPBH-TV Pittsburgh. He has disdain for his coworkers and viewers, but he has the most disdain for Groundhog Day held in Punxsutawney, Pennsylvania. He is scheduled to cover it for the third time in his career. Phil wants to get in and out of Punxsutawney as quickly as possible, but a snowstorm forces him to stay an extra night after the Groundhog Day festivities.

When Phil awakens the next morning, he experiences what he thinks is déjà vu. In reality, he is experiencing Groundhog Day in Punxsutawney all over again. The same thing happens the following day and for days after that.

Living an uninspired life is like this—filled with discontent, fear, worry, and frustration. Each day feels like a repeat of the day before, closed to possibility. It is as though life is being done to us, controlled by a force outside of ourselves rather than life being created, anew each and every day, actually each and every moment, through us.

When you are living an uninspired life your mind is closed to possibility and you are doomed to repeat the same patterns of thought, which generates (in-forms) your feelings and behavior, over and over and over again. You may have glimpses of hope but they are attached to an outside event or change of circumstance—a new job, weight loss, a birthday, marriage, birth of a child—or the hope that someone else will change—your spouse will stop drinking, your boss will appreciate you, your kids will be more communicative, your mom will stop criticizing you—and then life will be perfect.

Susyn believed that her misery and unhappiness would end when she was rescued by her knight in shining armor. Here is her story:

I used to think that my life would be perfect, filled with possibility and happily ever after once I got married. My anxiety, discontent, frustration, and fear would dissolve in the presence of my husband's love. I thought that if a man married me, all my problems, all my self-doubts would magically dissolve. And guess what? While there were certainly moments of joy and love in my former marriage, over time, my beliefs of not being loved, my uninspired deep-rooted programming, got hold of the steering wheel of my life.

Rather than seeing myself as being loved I both consciously and unconsciously convinced my husband that I was not lovable. I viewed his behavior toward me through my self-deprecating beliefs unaware of the role my beliefs were playing in my misery. I was living an uninspired life. Not because the outside circumstances were horrific, but rather because my thoughts, beliefs, assumptions, and choices were direct reflections of my feelings about myself. I felt victimized and uninspired by life.

Our lives are short, we live in the dash between the date we are born and the date we die. As adults, we have the choice to live an inspired life—awake to the possibility alive in each moment. So what do you choose, a Groundhog Day kind of existence, or an inspired life, lived from an unconditional loving relationship with yourself, and aligned with your true purpose, your heart's desire, your big dreams?

BREAKDOWNS:
BLOCKS, BARRIERS, AND OBSTACLES

Life's ups and downs provide windows of opportunity to determine your values and goals. Think of using all obstacles as stepping-stones to build the life you want.

—Marsha Sinetar

Have you ever noticed how blocks, barriers, and obstacles have a habit of popping up in your daily life? It may be as simple as forgetting where you've put your keys and suddenly your plans to leave the house to get to your long-awaited job interview, on time, are interrupted. In a moment, confident, ready-to-put-your-best-foot-forward you is frustrated. If you listen to your self-talk in the midst of your frustration, you may hear something like, *"Ugh! No matter what I do, things get screwed up,"* or *"Why does this always happen to me? I can't find my damn keys."*

Of course there may be more serious challenges that stop you in your tracks: death of a loved one, illness, a divorce, and in the midst of an economic crisis you may suddenly be out of work, unable to pay your monthly bills, questioning if you'll be able to stay in your home and how you will afford medical treatment, if needed.

Blocks, barriers, obstacles, and challenges are all part of life. No matter what the specific barrier blocking your path, it is on your path. It is the meaning you give to the obstacle and your reactions to it that either contribute to ongoing misery, suffering, frustration, fear, and hopelessness or offer you an opportunity to wake up and breathe life into your inspired life. Either way you are right. Your mind justifies any point of view. The glass is half empty or half full. One reaction stops you in your tracks and another offers possibilities.

I wonder, what if the glass being half empty and the glass being half full are both gateways to possibility? In Eastern cultures, an empty glass provides an open, womb-like space where new possibilities are birthed. In Western cultures, a half-full glass is a metaphor for success and accomplishment. Another way to think about this is that Eastern cultures represent a feminine way of seeing the world. Western cultures are rooted in a masculine perspective. Both offer possibility—they are different ways of defining possibility. When combined, opportunity abounds with the feminine energy generating possibility and the masculine energy moving effortlessly in the world through focused action.

When you are living an inspired life, you use blocks, barriers, and obstacles to:

- ❀ Wake up from the trance of life on automatic and appreciate what you do have.

- ❀ Acknowledge the fear, anger, frustration, and anxiety associated with your current situation and tap into your inner resources and the outer support of family, friends, community, and professionals.

- ❀ Unconditionally love the part of you that is suffering—listen to what that younger wounded part of you is feeling and what she or he needs. From the deeper, wider, connected center of your adult perspective, love that part of you.

- ❀ Detach and let go of the way you think things should be and be present to what is.

- ❀ Ask, *"What do I want?"* and *listen* to the answer.

- ❀ Take action.

Remember: Taking action only after you have connected with the deeper, wider part of you that has access to your inner wisdom and inner knowing—the part of you that experiences the world through a spiritual perspective— transforms breakdowns into breakthroughs.

In the next chapters we explore the common blocks and obstacles that stop us in our tracks and can derail an inspired life. As you read about them, become aware of the ones that apply to you, keeping in mind that each breakdown is an opportunity to explore your limiting beliefs about yourself, your relationships, and life that are standing in the way of and constricting the full flourishing of your inspired life. Welcome these blocks and obstacles as the opportunities that they are to upgrade the software of your mind.

> *An inspired life is knowing that even though you put one dream on hold to live another doesn't mean it's been forgotten. It's realizing that your weaknesses don't make you a failure but learning from them makes you a success. It's enjoying every moment and having a positive effect on at least one person every day! And it's letting the people you love know how much you appreciate them in your life.*
>
> *—Nina McPherson*

FEAR—MOVING THROUGH TO BREAK THROUGH

The key to change...is to let go of fear.
—*Rosanne Cash*

Fear is a common obstacle that acts as high-performing brakes preventing you from even allowing yourself to articulate your dreams and live an inspired life. The voice of fear can keep you stuck and be a barrier to the creative juices of an inspired life, easily convincing you that:

❀ Things won't work, so why even attempt to pursue your dreams. (You will readily be given examples of all the times in the past when things didn't work out and possibly images of the future of things not working out, as evidence that *you are a loser.*)

❀ You're not smart enough so you might as well stay where you are: in the job, in the relationship, in the house, because you just aren't smart enough.

❀ It's not safe to be happy and enjoy yourself, because it's not going to last, so armor yourself up and protect yourself from future hurt and disappointment. (While it is true that all situations and circumstances are temporary and change, it does seem absurd to prevent yourself from enjoying the present moment because it will not last forever!)

The spirit of fear is love inverted, or your own mental power turned against yourself.
—Marianne Williamson

We have found it helpful to think of the word fear as an acronym. Here are few examples you can choose from:

False	**F**ailure	**F**inding	**F**orgetting
Evidence	**E**xpected	**E**xcuses	**E**verything is
Appearing	**A**nd	**A**nd	**A**ll
Real	**R**eceived	**R**easons	**R**ight

In order to harness the potent energy present in fear, in addition to reframing the meaning you give to the circumstance that evoked fear, you must face it with your vision of your inspired life in mind. Katie Freiling is an online marketing and personal growth educator and speaker. She is a pioneer in video blogging, but first had to face her fear of public speaking in order to step into her inspired life.

Here is Katie's story:

My biggest fear, without a doubt, was public speaking. The mere thought of it made my body quiver and my stomach nauseous. It is the one thing I dreaded the most! The first time I was asked by my company to fly to Las Vegas and speak in front of about 150 people I was scared to death. I tried to hide my fear as I walked to the front of the room with the microphone in hand.

As I started speaking, my throat constricted and it was very hard to breathe. All of a sudden my heart was beating out of my chest. I was convinced that everyone could hear it through the microphone! Like a deer in headlights, my mind completely blanked on the speech I had prepared. An overwhelming feeling of weakness flowed throughout my body. I realized I was about to faint! My knees started buckling. Before I hit the ground, I ran back to my seat and held my head down before I went unconscious.

I was absolutely humiliated. I wanted to shrivel up into a little ball and disappear. Thankfully everyone around me was very understanding and compassionate. They did their best to make me feel better. That day was one of the most embarrassing and one of the most growth-producing opportunities of my life!

I knew I needed to overcome my fear of public speaking if I wanted to fully step into my own power. So when my company asked me to speak again in Orlando,

Florida, I had to say yes. My mind was resisting it and I was tempted to start coming up with any excuse I could think of to not do it. But my heart was telling me that this was important. I needed this chance to truly detach from my biggest fear and really walk the walk when it comes to personal growth and development.

The morning of my speech, I spent some time alone, in my room, and did some deep breathing. I sat there with my eyes closed and envisioned myself walking onto the stage with confidence and power. In my mind, when I looked out to see the crowd of people staring back at me, I felt completely and utterly free. I consciously invoked the feeling of freedom—free from all fear. Instead of fearing another awful scenario, I consciously chose to focus on feeling empowered and free. There was no way I was going to sabotage myself by creating mental pictures of what I didn't want. I mentally rehearsed the outcome of what I did want.

After getting grounded and centered, I made my way down to the event. There were about four hundred people in the audience. When my name was called, I walked to the podium smiling. As I looked at the audience, I remembered what I had practiced—feeling empowered and free when I saw everyone looking back at me.

Instead of focusing on how I looked or what others thought, I chose to focus on what I could give to my audience. The more I spoke, the more the words flowed. When

I finished and walked backstage, I was greeted with big hugs from everyone, most of whom had heard about the "incident" in Las Vegas. I felt so relieved and really proud of myself. I did it! I overcame my biggest fear!

INSPIRED LIFE ACTION: TRANSFORM YOUR FEAR

Focus your attention on something that evokes fear in you. Following Katie's example, allow yourself some quiet time. Take a few full deep breaths and then write a description of yourself as confident and empowered as you face and move through the situation that previously evoked fear. Once your description is written, close your eyes, and, using the full resources of your imagination create a scene of your desired result fully accomplished. Step into the scene and experience your success.

Remember: While fear can automatically stop you in your tracks, it can serve as a powerful wake-up call. Fear reminds you that it is the thoughts you are thinking, the meaning you endow circumstances with, and the programming that is running you, not the actual situation that is your primary obstacle.

CONQUER YOUR AUTOMATIC RESPONSES TO FEAR

Your FEAR signature is how you experience fear in your body and thoughts. To identify your FEAR signature, respond to the following questions:

1. When you are feeling fearful, where in your body do you experience these feelings? (For example, heart palpitations, shallow breathing, neck, shoulder, and lower back pain, knots in your stomach, grinding your teeth, etc.)

2. When you are feeling fearful, what thoughts are repeated in your mind? (For example, "Nothing works for me. I don't know how to do this. I'm not (fill in the blank) enough. I'm afraid if I'm successful that my friends and family will think that I'm snobby," and so on.)

3. When you are feeling fearful, what words do you speak? (For example, "I guess the universe is telling me that this is not the right path for me. Yeah, yeah, I know that thoughts create my reality but this is different. This is just the way I am, and how things always work for me...")

4. When you are feeling fearful, what actions do you take? (For example, overeating or other addictive behaviors, withdrawing and isolating, stopping exercising, deciding to take steps tomorrow and failing to follow through, etc...)

With an awareness of your FEAR signature you will now more readily notice when fear is creeping into your experience. As soon as you notice this, focus your attention on a F.E.A.R. acronym described earlier to intervene in your automatic fear response. Once you have intervened:

❀ Ask yourself, *What would I like to have happen in this situation?* What is your intention or your desired result?

❀ With your intention in mind, ask yourself, *What is my next step?* Listen to the answer and take action.

❀ If you continue to feel stuck, ask for help from someone you know who has been successful in moving through fear, or a coach, trusted advisor, or therapist.

ANXIETY AND WORRY—
A WAKE-UP CALL TO AWARENESS

Worry is a thin stream of fear trickling through the mind. If encouraged, it cuts a channel into which all other thoughts are drained.

—Arthur Somers Roche

Anxiety and worry, like fear, are powerful obstacles on the path to living an inspired life. You may worry about your upcoming job interview not going well. You may be anxious about whether you can afford to keep your house. You may worry that your kids are addicted to drugs. Your anxiety about a persistent stomach pain may be so debilitating that you don't seek professional advice. You may be so consumed with worry that your spouse is going to have an affair that there is no space for you to be loving in your relationship.

Whatever the circumstance or situation that triggers your anxiety and worry, the *thoughts* you have about those situations and the *meaning* you give to those circumstances are the true blocks and barriers to living an inspired life.

Consciously choosing to focus your attention on the powerful mantra, *Thoughts Create,* is a potent antidote when you are overwhelmed with worry and anxiety. Yes, it is true that things do not always work out the way you thought they should but anxiety and worry detract from your peace of mind and constrict your ability to focus your attention on moving forward and transforming the roadblocks into stepping-stones.

Use your awareness of your feelings of worry and anxiety as a springboard to wake up to your thoughts and then tap into the creative resources of your inspired life vision to think thoughts that focus on what you desire, not what you are worried about. A simple model to follow is to fill in the blanks in the following statement:

When I am feeling _____,
I am believing _____.

If your eyes are blinded with your worries you cannot see the beauty of the sunset.
—Jiddu Krishnamurti

Eric was a coaching client who suffered with severe anxiety for as long as he could remember. He felt nervous all the time and would go through bouts of sleeplessness for months at a time. After six months of this he was often having suicidal thoughts. He searched the Internet for information to help relieve his anxiety. The more information he got, the more worried he became. Would he ever be free of his anxiety—would he ever sleep through the night and wake up rested?

He thought about seeing a therapist but his embarrassment and shame only increased his anxiety. He actually made a few appointments and cancelled them. He prayed and hoped that God would intervene but when his sleepless nights continued he worried that God had abandoned him and hadn't heard his prayers.

After six sleepless months he courageously called our office and made an appointment that he kept. During our first session he agreed to acknowledge his anxiety, free of judgments, to stop focusing all his attention and energy on his anxiety, and to begin to enjoy his life. He made a list of thoughts that brought him a sense of calm and activities he enjoyed. After a few weeks, he reported, "Once I began to focus on having a good time and appreciating and enjoying my life, slowly I was able to sleep a few hours at a time."

After nine months, during our last session Eric told me, "Anxiety is tricky. The more I tried to get rid of it the worse it became. When I finally acknowledged that I was anxious, stopped trying to get rid of it, and focused my attention on what I enjoyed, it seemed as though I had discovered a magic solution. The key was to *stop* fighting my anxiety. Acknowledge it without judgments, listen to, connect with, and soothe the anxious part of me and then fill my mind with satisfying thoughts and do things I like to do. If I'd waited for the anxiety to disappear before I started to be grateful and enjoy my life, I'd still be waiting and fighting to be rid of the anxiety while I continued to be immersed in it. When I focused on enjoying life, my anxiety was transformed!"

INSPIRED LIFE ACTION: CREATE A PLEASURE LIST

Create a "pleasure list" of the people, places, things, and activities that bring you pleasure, put a smile on your face and warm your heart when you think about them or when you do them. Keep your list in a place where you can see it. When you notice anxiety and worry knocking on your door, acknowledge them and then focus your thoughts and actions on items on your pleasure list. Notice your attitude change. Shifting your focus, even for a moment, to something you enjoy sends a clear message to your brain: *"I choose where I focus my attention"* and *"I am in control of my thoughts and feelings."* When you practice this activity you strengthen your commitment to living in alignment with your inspired life vision.

Mary Angela Buffo is the owner and director of Ananda Yoga and Wellness Center in Southampton, New York. We were out for a walk one day, talking about worry when she shared her "creating a worry-free zone" idea with me. Here is her story:

*I had been tossing and turning one night, unable to stop
what seemed to be an endless tape playing and replaying
in my mind. One worry-filled thought after another took
center stage in my thoughts. I'd visited another yoga center
earlier in the day and saw some of my old clients there—
clients who were no longer attending my classes. As I lay
in bed I was counting the money I had lost since these
students were no longer enrolled in classes at Ananda.*

*Worries of not having enough money to meet my
expenses were filling my mind as an unending restless-
ness had me tossing and turning. I did my best to remind
myself that Ananda, in its tenth year, had just had its best
summer ever! My bills were paid and there was money in
the bank.*

*But I couldn't free my mind, for more than a few
minutes at a time, from this worry. After a few hours I
left my bedroom and went downstairs to the living room.
I made myself comfortable on the couch and asked the
question, "How can I free myself of this worry?" As I sat
with my eyes closed, when my mind wandered to thoughts
that fueled worry I redirected my attention to the question, "How can I free myself of this worry?"*

*After about ten minutes I heard the words, "Make your
bedroom a worry-free zone. No worries in your bedroom."
I liked this idea and decided to experiment. If worries
popped into my mind when I was in the bedroom, I would
leave the room so it would be my worry-free sanctuary.*

Within a few minutes I went back upstairs to my bedroom and declared, "Bedroom, you are a worry-free zone!"

Since that day there have been times when I have had to leave my bedroom since worry was making itself comfortable in my mind. I'd stand outside the bedroom and read the sign I had made and hung on the door, "WORRY-FREE ZONE." I'd take a few deep breaths and step through the door, and feel the safety and comfort of my worry-free sanctuary.

Is it time for you to create a worry-free sanctuary in your home?

REGRET: LET GO AND LIVE IN THE PRESENT

> *When one door closes, another opens; but we often look so long and so regretfully upon the closed door that we do not see the one which has opened for us.*
>
> —*Alexander Graham Bell*

Regret about what you did or didn't do, said or didn't say, can capture you in a tangled web which can feel as though you are stuck in fast-drying cement. Using the full resources of your imagination you are so caught up in wishing things in the past had been different that you forego the opportunity for happiness and joy in the present. This is a simple recipe for an uninspired life.

Susyn was lost in a tangled web of regret that often felt like a prison. Here's her story:

After eleven years together my marriage ended when my husband announced, during a phone call, that he had filed for divorce. A few days earlier we had had a screaming match after he told me he had decided not to discipline one of the kids.

It was the same old story, one of the kids had been irresponsible—he'd left the dogs out in a thunderstorm, and the front door of the house wide open when he'd gone out for the afternoon. Dan and I had agreed upon the consequence and he had promised to talk with David and ground him for two weeks.

I was feeling as though we were finally on the same page with the kids. But while I was out exercising, Dan changed his mind, as usual! When I returned home and asked him how his conversation with David had gone, he said, "I decided not to discipline him, the dogs were okay, and we weren't robbed when the door was left opened." I was furious and the yelling began.

Two days later Dan filed for divorce.

I spent countless hours during the next year wishing I hadn't gotten into what turned out to be the final argument of our marriage. With regret causing pains in my stomach, in my imagination I was constantly attempting to change the past with "if onlys": if only I hadn't gotten so angry; if only David hadn't left the dogs out and the door open; if only I hadn't stormed out of the house; if only...if only...if only.

After seemingly endless months of tear-filled days and nights and much wishing and hoping, it was clear that Dan was determined to go through with the divorce. With the support of loving friends, talented therapists, and a local 12-Step Program, it became quite evident that

I could not change the circumstances of the past. What I could do was free myself of the regret that was causing my present misery.

Once I committed to detaching from my debilitating feelings of regret—the endless litany of "if onlys"—and evolving my thinking, my daily life s-l-o-w-l-y became bearable and eventually pleasurable. Over time I was able to see my marriage, not through the eyes of loss, but rather remembering the opportunities it offered me to learn about and experience love.

As with all these blocks, barriers, and obstacles it is through healing your mind, the thoughts you think, the programming that runs you, and the meaning you give to the circumstances before you that you are able to tap into the creative resources of your inspired life. Using the power inherent in the present moment is your direct access to creating the life you desire—a life that truly honors the precious present as a gift.

An inspired life is one that is lived with intention, being fully present each moment so that if we look back there would be no regrets.

—Calla Crafts

INSPIRED MIND PRACTICE: AFFIRM YOURSELF

When you notice that you have been seduced by regret and "if onlys" have captured your attention, use the following mantra to detach and let go of your misery: "I did the best that I could based on my thinking at that time. I choose to focus my attention on the present with gratitude."

Remember: Focusing on past regrets not only drains your energy but also robs you of the possibility of joy in the present.

IDENTIFY THE GIFTS

Every situation in our life offers us the opportunity to learn about ourselves. When you notice you are caught in the web of regret, ask yourself, "What did I learn from this situation about my beliefs about myself, others, and life? What are the gifts of this situation?"

EXPECTATIONS: CHOOSING A NEW THOUGHT

I am not in this world to live up to other people's expectations, nor do I feel that the world must live up to mine.

—Fritz Perls

Expectations that you place on yourself and others create a natural pathway to disappointment. Expectations are filled with *shoulds* and *oughts* limiting what is possible. Unmet expectations are viewed as failures resulting in feelings of disappointment, anger, and a sense of victimization.

Expectations are simply thoughts that you have about the way you *think* things should be or how you *think* someone, including yourself, ought to act. Since they are actually thoughts, you have the freedom to create and consciously choose a new thought that is more satisfying for you and others who are involved in the situation.

Here is a list of some ordinary expectations that can create chaos in your life:

❀ If you really loved me, you would know what I'm thinking and feeling.

❀ If you really loved me, you would help me without my having to ask you for help.

❀ If you really loved me, you would agree with my point of view.

❀ If you cared about me, you wouldn't disappoint me.

❀ If I want it done right, I'd better do it myself.

❀ Love won't last.

❀ I can't count on people to help me.

In terms of expectations, an important question to ask yourself is, *"Do I want to be right or do I want to be happy?"* If you truly desire happiness and an inspired life then you have to be willing to:

- ❀ understand that at each and every moment everyone is doing the very best they can based on *their* programming;

- ❀ acknowledge that while expectations may offer you a direction to go in they are not etched in stone;

- ❀ be open to opportunities and spontaneous possibilities along the way allowing the creative juices of an inspired life to flow.

Joan's story demonstrates the destructive power of expectations.

I was raised in an upper middle class Jewish family with the expectations that I would be married in my twenties to a man who was college educated, came from an excellent Jewish family, and worked hard to make a great living. We would live in New York and raise a nice Jewish family.

My twenties were filled with many unsatisfying rela-

tionships. I was always looking for the "perfect" guy to meet the expectations that had been programmed into me from the time I was a child by my family. When I did date a man who matched this list of expectations he either did not have time for me because he was too busy with his career or I simply didn't like him.

One day, when I was thirty-two, I was sitting in my New York City apartment feeling depressed and hopeless. I was thinking if only I could find a guy to support me in the style I was accustomed, I would be happy. I wanted a great guy who had time for me and who was wealthy. We would live on Sutton Place in New York City in a beautiful apartment overlooking the East River.

As I was thinking these thoughts, I kept getting more and more depressed because my reality in no way matched my expectations. I decided to sit down and write in my journal. As I started to write what I was feeling I had an inspired moment.

What I really wanted was a guy who had time to spend with me, someone I could laugh with and be myself with. Why did he have to be Jewish? College educated? Etc.? And if I wanted an apartment overlooking the East River, why did I need a man to provide it? It was at that moment that I realized my expectations were holding me back from what I really wanted. This inspired moment changed my life. I embraced what I truly wanted, not what I thought I should have, not the way I thought it should look.

Soon after this inspired moment I met Bruce, a widower with five kids, no college degree, who was ready to retire from a civil service job and sail around the world. We fell in love. I was living my inspired life, free of the expectations that were actually blocking my happiness. We sailed together for four years. When we stopped sailing, I came back to New York City and created a multimillion dollar business.

Today, twenty-seven years later, we are still happily married. And we live in a house with a beautiful water view!

INSPIRED LIFE EXERCISE: LETTING GO OF EXPECTATIONS
Complete the following sentence with as many responses as come to mind: In order to be happy, I should_____

_____

_____

_____.

You have just defined your expectations. Now complete the following sentence free of *shoulds* and *oughts*: My dream life is_____

_____

_____

_____.

What do you notice? What's keeping you from detaching and letting go of your expectations?

Remember: Your expectations of how you think your life should be, how you think your life should look, may be exactly what are blocking you from happiness.

IF YOU LISTEN, YOUR HEART WILL TELL YOU WHAT YOU WANT

Whenever you are feeling disappointed, ask yourself, "What do I want in this situation?" Listen to the answer. Follow the guidance. Be willing to allow life to give you a present, which may not look like what you expect, but is more satisfying than you could have ever imagined!

If you want to have an expectation, experiment with this: Trust that when you declare a clear intention the path to its fulfillment is being illuminated step-by-step.

JUDGMENTS: BE OPEN TO NEW PERSPECTIVES

If you judge people, you have no time to love them.

—*Mother Teresa*

Judgments are barriers that separate and divide people. If you judge that someone is like you based on gender, age, race, education, financial status, religion, politics, sexual orientation, or any other category you can think of, then you feel connected with them. When you judge others as different from you then it is easy to think less of them, hate them through your criticism, or kill them in actual battle.

Judgments enable you to easily forget that all beings spring from a common source and that we are connected simply in that we are living and breathing the same air at the same time on the same planet.

Judgments about yourself lead to low self-esteem, fear, self-loathing, and self-abuse in words and behavior. It is these thoughts and judgments that are the true barriers and obstacles to allowing yourself to live an inspired life and to take actions that would nourish your dreams.

Some of your judgments may be so automatic and seamless that you don't even realize you are engaged in the act of judging. For instance, have you ever gotten up in the morning and as you were brushing your teeth and looking at yourself in the mirror your thoughts went something like this, *"I look disgusting. I'm just plain ugly. My hair is a mess. Ugh, I have a zit. I hate the way I look."* These judgments, declared with conviction, are a powerful form of abuse. This is a form of domestic violence, where you are the perpetrator, doing harm to yourself through your thoughts.

These judgments of your ego-mind literally Edge God Out and prevent you from nourishing, nurturing, and living an inspired life.

The following teaching story demonstrates how judgments blind us to a new perspective, a new point of view that may be right before our eyes.

THE WONDERFUL CRACKED POT
Traditional Story from India adapted by Dan Gibson

A water bearer in India had two large pots, each hung on one end of a pole, which he carried across his neck. One of the pots had a crack in it, while the other pot was perfect and always delivered a full portion of water at the end of the long walk from the stream to the master's house. The cracked pot arrived only half full.

For a full two years this went on daily, with the bearer delivering only one-and-a-half pots full of water to his master's house. Of course, the perfect pot was proud of its accomplishments. But the poor cracked pot was ashamed of its own imperfection and miserable that it was able to accomplish only half of what it had been made to do. After two years of what it judged to be a bitter failure, it spoke to the water bearer one day by the stream.

"I am ashamed of myself, and I want to apologize to you."

"Why?" asked the bearer. "What are you ashamed of?"

"I have been able, for these past two years, to deliver only half my load because this crack in my side causes water to leak out all the way back to your master's house. Because of my flaws, you have to do all of this work, and you don't get full value from your efforts," the pot said.

The water bearer felt sorry for the old cracked pot, and in his compassion he said, "As we return to the master's house, I want you to notice the beautiful flowers along the path." Indeed, as they went up the hill, the old cracked pot took notice of the sun warming the beautiful wildflowers on the side of the path, and this cheered it some. But at the end of the trail, it still felt bad because it had leaked out half its load, and so again the pot apologized to the bearer for its failure.

The bearer said to the pot, "Did you notice that there were flowers only on your side of the path, but not on the other pot's side? That's because I have always known about your flaw, and I took advantage of it. I planted flower seeds on your side of the path, and every day while we walk back from the stream, you've watered them. For two years I have been able to pick these beautiful flowers and to decorate my master's table. Without you being just the way you are, he would not have this beauty to grace his house.

INSPIRED LIFE PRACTICE: TRANSFORMING YOUR JUDGMENTS

Use this exercise to heighten your awareness of making judgments and then transforming them in the present moment. When you catch yourself making judgments *don't*, we repeat, *don't judge yourself for judging*! Acknowledge yourself for noticing your judgmental thoughts. Say, "Ooops" and refocus your attention on thoughts that consciously inspire you to be a mighty expression of love in the world.

Remember: All judgments, whether positive or negative, create separation. This is good, that is bad. This is right, that is wrong. At every moment, everyone's words and actions are a seamless reflection of their dominant brain pathways.

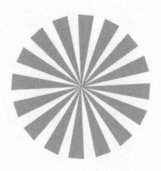

TRACK YOUR JUDGING

Experiment for one day to become aware of the number of judgments you make about yourself, others, the weather, the government, etc. Every time you notice you are making a judgment—whether it is *this is good* or *that is bad*—put a check mark on a piece of paper or on your smartphone notepad. Are you surprised by the number of judgmental thoughts that passed through your mind during one day?

Up the ante: do this for seven days and for each judgment you make place a quarter in a container. How much money have you saved by the end of the week?

ADDICTIONS: GO FROM HABITUAL TO HAPPINESS

Addictions block you from fully accessing your creative resources because you feel powerless in their presence.

—Sheri Rosenthal

Addictions are any habitual psychological and/or physiological dependence on substances, thoughts, behaviors, or practices that you cannot easily control. The automatic obsessive thinking and compulsive behavior resulting from your addictions leave little room for making the conscious creative choices that are the hallmarks of an inspired life.

We tend to look at addiction from a limited point of view, focusing on typical addictions like drugs, alcohol, food, sex, smoking, exercise, gambling, shopping, and work. It is obvious that these addictive habits can and do create obstacles in all aspects of life.

It is also crucial to understand that there are other addictions, mental addictions, which are subtler than a specific substance or behavior, and are deadly in terms of your self-esteem and joyfulness. These are addictions to habits of thinking that result in ongoing misery and suffering. Here are some examples:

❀ If you cannot stop arguing with the people you love, you are addicted to your opinions and judgments.

❀ If you cannot end your self-deprecating internal dialogue, you are addicted to self-hate.

❀ If you cannot forgive those you are angry with, you are addicted to resentment.

❀ If you cannot cease making a big deal out of everything, you are addicted to drama.

❀ If you cannot discontinue your need to be right and make others wrong, you are addicted to pride.

❀ If you cannot prevent yourself from replaying negative self-talk, you are addicted to incessant abusive internal dialogue.

❀ If you cannot stop talking about yourself, you are addicted to self-importance.

❀ If you cannot stop self-sabotaging behaviors, you are addicted to failure.

❀   If you cannot end your need for painful relationships, you are addicted to victimization.

The good news is that once you see that you are addicted
to so many harmful thoughts and actions, you can change
these patterns. These changes begin by creating new brain
pathways that access inspired wisdom and acknowledge the
power inherent in the statement, *Thoughts Create Reality*.

Lee McCormick is the founder of The Ranch Recovery
Center, but before recovery, being an addict was more
than a diagnosis for him. Here is Lee's story:

*In the beginning, I was told and believed that I was
somehow not normal. Addiction was not just a diagnosis;
it was a definition that came immediately after my name.
"Hello, my name is Lee, and I'm an addict."*

*I was told that if I did not live always conscious of my
disease—addiction—I would be lost in suffering, mental
illness, or death. I learned that I needed to ask forgiveness
from all those I had harmed. What I wasn't taught was to
forgive myself. Someone had to be wrong, and I was the
one on trial. There was no forgiveness in that scenario
and no chance to change the thinking that resulted in my
excessive drug use in the first place.*

*Forgiveness was the answer, but not coming from my
self-judgment and guilt. Once I took responsibility for my
actions without judgments, I forgave because I wanted to*

free myself, from suffering and guilt, as a gift of self-love and respect. In addition to freeing myself from my addiction to drugs I discovered total freedom from my deadly habits of self-berating stories of being less-than and not good enough.

INSPIRED LIFE EXERCISE:
IDENTIFY AUTOMATIC THOUGHTS AND CHANGE SELF-DEFEATING BEHAVIOR

Use this exercise to free yourself of the mental addictions that create blocks, barriers, and obstacles to living an inspired life. Choose an addiction you would like to be free of and do the following: Observe it. Make a list of the real reasons behind the addiction. In other words, what are you telling yourself to justify your actions? For instance, if you are a workaholic, do you believe that the only way to get ahead and to be appreciated and validated is by being a workaholic? If this is your belief then you will continue this addiction until you realize that it is through loving and appreciating yourself—through self-love— that true validation is experienced.

Imagine yourself free of your addiction. What are the thoughts you would be thinking about yourself when these mental addictions no longer consume your time and energy? Make a list of not-doings—actions you can take to free yourself of the compulsive behavior associated with the addiction. For example, if you tend to talk about yourself incessantly, a not-doing would be to listen rather than talk during a conversation, or ask questions about the topic the other person is talking about.

Blocks, barriers, and obstacles pop up in life. It is your reaction to them, based on the meaning you give to them, that is of primary importance in either fueling them or freeing yourself from them.

Remember: An inspired mind is free of obsessive thoughts and compulsive behaviors that are inherent in addictions. When living an inspired life you are free to use the full resources of your imagination to create and live in your vision of fulfillment.

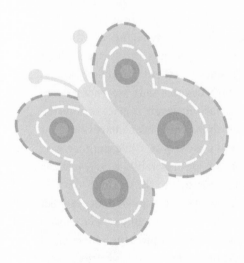

AVOIDANCE: STOPPING SELF-SABOTAGE

If you want to get from point A to point B you cannot avoid starting where you are.

Avoidance is known by many names: pretending, procrastinating, lying, suppressing, and evading. It is a strategy that is developed as a way of protecting ourselves from challenging and painful feelings, which are related to our feelings of inadequacy and our embodied anticipation, expressed as fear and anxiety, of less than our desired results.

I assume you are all familiar with avoidance of a difficult conversation or topic, as sometimes it is like a pink elephant in the room. Everyone knows it is there, but the obvious is never expressed. Not only does this separate people from authentic connection—it has the deadly impact of severing our connection with ourselves. There is one part of us that is acting as though nothing is wrong, while another part of us—on the inside—is feeling miserable, angry, just the opposite of what we are presenting to the world.

When avoidance is our primary strategy to dodge conflict and sidestep expressing ourselves authentically we lose contact with our inner truth, our vision of an inspired life. Our connection with the Greater Field of Life becomes constricted.

. Let me be clear, there are times when avoidance is the perfect strategy:

🏵 When you need time and patience to get clear about your vision and your next step aligned with your intention.

🏵 When other people are involved and you allow the time for them to work it out. (This can be a useful strategy, for parents when their children are having a disagreement, between coworkers when you're the boss but don't use this as an excuse to justify your default avoidance strategy!)

🏵 When your habitual approach to circumstances of life is ready-aim-fire, avoidance provides the opportunity to take a step back and consciously choose the action that supports your desired result.

There are times when avoidance is not readily apparent, as in this story of Susyn's coaching client, Angela:

A classic workaholic, Angela was a forty-one-year-old, divorced, successful business owner. Her day began at six am for an hour at the gym—armed with her iPad opened for work. Angela's workday usually ended about ten-thirty pm when she returned to her empty apartment, where three to four nights a week she worked for a few more hours. She was constantly plugged in to her phone— on the verge of a tantrum when her battery was speedily approaching empty and her charger wasn't in sight.

She often complained about having no social life, no time for her friends and family. Angela blamed time for this problem and didn't think she was responsible for the choices she made, rather she said during one session, "If I had more time then I would have a more balanced and satisfying life. My problem is simply that there aren't enough hours in the day!"

As our coaching sessions continued what became clear is that Angela's workaholic behavior was actually the perfect way for her to avoid the painful and unresolved feelings she had associated with intimate relationships. Her parents divorced when she was five years old and she saw and continues to see her father infrequently. She believes that her divorce, after a two-year marriage, is proof that she really can't count on a man to be with her forever. She is certain she will be abandoned, and as we explored a bit further she believed that she is unlovable. By working morning, noon, and night, Angela was able to successfully avoid close relationships—so she would not be abandoned. But here's the catch—while she was avoiding intimacy with others, she was also avoiding being honest with herself about her vision for her life; she was actually abandoning herself. She was often praised for her dedication to her work, while on the inside she was running as fast as she could to avoid really identifying her vision of an inspired life and her self-sabotaging beliefs and behavior.

With this awareness and Angela's commitment to free herself from the patterns of the past, she declared her desire to be part of a family and community of friends in addition to being a successful businesswoman. Within six months, Angela hired an assistant, started taking dancing lessons, committed to working overtime no more than one night per week, and was dating one of her dance partners.

With greater clarity about the beliefs you have about yourself, others, and life that generate a default avoidance pattern, you can consciously choose the best approach to take as you make choices based on your inspired life vision being fulfilled.

INSPIRED LIFE STRATEGY: STOP AVOIDING LIFE

Identify an area of your life where avoidance is your primary strategy. It might be: having a conversation with your boss about the additional work you are expected to complete due to downsizing; having a conversation with your spouse/partner about adding some spice to your sex life; talking with people at the bank who hold your mortgage about your fear of foreclosure; making a doctor's appointment about the discomfort you have been having in your chest for the past two months. Write your responses to the following questions:

❀ I avoid _____
(identify the situation)_____
____because_____
_____. Write for ten minutes, allowing yourself to write whatever comes to your mind, free of judgment.

❀ My intention for this situation is_____
_____(the result you desire)_____
_____?

❀ In order to evolve my avoidance pattern, I commit to_____
and allow support from_____
_____.

❀ Take action.

Remember: Avoidance can be a useful strategy, allowing you time to gather more information, become clear regarding your intention, and determine your next step, but when it is your default strategy, it erodes the fulfillment of living an inspired life.

UNCERTAINTY: BEING PRESENT TO YOUR OWN LIFE

Uncertainty and mystery are energies of life. Don't let them scare you unduly, for they keep boredom at bay and spark creativity.

—R. I. Fitzhenry

Uncertainty often stops people in their tracks. Most people are on a constant search for certainty, wanting to know that this relationship will last forever, or this business idea is a sure winner, or this diet is "the one" that will finally get them to their perfect weight forever, once and for all. But life is uncertain, forever evolving, and in general the only thing we can be sure of is uncertainty.

While the spark of creativity that uncertainty generates is fuel for living an inspired life, all too often the discomfort, anxiety, and fear experienced in the presence of uncertainty can be paralyzing, keeping people stuck in situations which are really not satisfying but are comfortable in their familiarity.

Susyn tells the story of one of her clients whose uncertainty became a stepping stone to clarity:

Andy was in the throes of misery and unhappiness when he came for his first coaching appointment. During the past two years his marriage had become one long argument. There seemed to be no topic that was safe for him and his wife to discuss without an ensuing confrontation. The loving relationship that marked their courtship and early marriage was difficult for him to recall and their sex life was nonexistent. As he described his unhappiness, he declared, "But as uncomfortable as this is and as unhappy as I am, I am more anxious and fearful about making a change. How can I be certain that a new relationship, a new job, or a new city will be any better?"

He was right; he couldn't be certain what the future would hold if he were to make changes. What he could be certain of is that if he didn't make a change the well-trodden path of unhappiness would continue. With this in mind he came up with a list of options: separating from his wife, seeing if he could transfer to another job in his company in another city, having a real conversation with his wife, sharing his unhappiness and his desire to rekindle their love, starting the business he was waiting to start when he retires in another twenty-five years, having a baby in hopes that this would bring the needed change to his marriage. As he shared his list with me, after an initial boost of energy his fears emerged. He wanted to be certain that he would make the right choice and was afraid that he didn't know what that was. During one session he actually said, "Can't you just tell me what to do?" And while I didn't have one of the answers he was expecting: "No, I can't tell you," or "Yes, this is what you should do," I did have an answer for him, "Before you can decide your next step there are two things you have to do:

1. *Create a clear vision of the life you desire, and*
2. *Transform your relationship with uncertainty."*

There is a happy ending to Andy's story. He made a vision board during one of our sessions and by getting "out of his head" and allowing his creativity free rein, his vision of his inspired life became clearer. He was eager to share this with his wife, but his uncertainty about her response stopped him in his tracks for a while. He decided to invite her to one of our coaching sessions to share his vision board with her. She agreed. Although he was uncertain of her response, he didn't allow that to stop him from authentically communicating his desires to his wife during their coaching session. To his surprise, she said that she would like to make a vision board and share it with him. Within eight months their marriage transformed and Andy made plans to start his own business with his wife's encouragement and support.

Life is continually evolving and when you can accept that you are feeling uncertain, and not judge or fight it a clear direction and next step will surface. It is crucial to keep in mind there is always a way through, around, under, or over the blocks and obstacles that show up in your life. If they are present, it does not mean that you are doomed to an uninspired life, rather they are a potent invitation for you to stop, survey the territory, focus on your inspired life vision, and with that in mind ask, "What is my next step?" It is when you use blocks and obstacles as judgments or evidence that you are a victim and not worthy of happiness, fulfillment, and joy that you become imprisoned in an uninspired life.

INSPIRED LIFE GAME: YOU MIGHT REALLY KNOW

This is a simple mind game that I often use with clients— and with myself, as well. When I am uncertain of the next step to take, or the next decision to make, I ask myself: "What if I did know my next step, or the decision to make, what would it be?" Sometimes, by freeing my mind from not knowing and uncertainty, I open myself to possibility and ideas flow freely; other times I hear "be patient" and that is a reminder to allow time for the answer to be revealed.

Remember: Humans are meaning-making machines and it is the meaning you give to the circumstance of your life that determines if you are living an inspired or uninspired life.

PART FOUR:
SEEDS OF AN INSPIRED LIFE

LIVING AN INSPIRED LIFE

For me an inspired life is a combination of being focused, stimulated, and excited about what I am doing, combined with being productive and making a positive contribution to society.

—David Riklan

This section of the book introduces you to the ingredients of an inspired life. You may discover that you are familiar with some of these and quite adept at putting them into practice while others have been a challenge for you to implement consistently. And then there may be some ingredients that are completely new to you.

Whether or not you are familiar with all or some of the ingredients we encourage you to experiment with all of them, knowing that each one adds to the flavor, spice, and richness of your life and forms the fertile soil of an inspired life.

To provide context we begin with our operating principles. You may readily agree with them or you may be skeptical. Either way, we ask that you suspend judgment and explore the power of these principles as you cultivate and nourish your inspired life.

❀ Life is a co-creative partnership with the Greater Field of Life.

❀ Our thoughts, beliefs, feelings, choices, words, and actions are the tools we use to create our greatest masterpiece—our lives.

❀ By articulating and embodying a clear vision, the universe responds with a resounding YES and opportunities that nourish the fulfill-ment of our inspired life vision are revealed.

❀ By transforming our thinking, and the meaning we attach to the circumstances of our lives, we transform our experience.

❀ By nurturing a loving relationship with ourselves, we deepen and expand our capacity to live a loving, fulfilling, joyful, and happy life.

COMMIT FIRST: LIVING WITH PASSION AND PURPOSE

Our commitments are that which we orbit around. They are our sun, and they feed us the ability to organize our lives around that which is meaningful to us.

—*Katherine Woodward Thomas*

Living an inspired life starts with a commitment. Often we wait to make a commitment until we are certain that all the *i*'s are dotted and all the *t*'s are crossed. We hesitate in committing too soon, thinking: *"What if it doesn't work out? What if I can't do it?"* Fear and anxiety can go into overdrive when faced with making a commitment. Yet, the reality of the creative process is just the opposite and requires that we commit first. The words of W. H. Murray (1951 Scottish Himalayan Expedition) describe the power of committing first:

Until one is committed, there is hesitancy, the chance to draw back, always ineffectiveness. Concerning all acts of initiative (and creation), there is one elementary truth the ignorance of which kills countless ideas and splendid plans: that the moment one definitely commits oneself, then providence moves too. A whole stream of events issues from the decision, raising in one's favor all manner of unforeseen incidents, meetings, and material assistance, which no man could have dreamt would have come his way. I learned a deep respect for one of Goethe's couplets:

"Whatever you can do, or dream you can, begin it. Boldness has genius, power and magic in it!"

A commitment is sometimes born in a spurt of inspiration when your passion is ignited, an idea explodes in your mind fully formed, and every cell of your being harmonizes in a resounding *Yes*. Or a commitment is made when you are f*@king tired of feeling miserable. You are so clear about what you don't want that, in the words of Abraham, through Esther Hicks, you experience *a rocket of desire* and you think, *"Yes, I'm gonna do this!"* so you make a New Year's resolution, a birthday wish, a new moon intention, or you decide that today is the first day of the rest of your life.

It is important to be clear about what you are committing to. We are used to thinking that what we are committing to is the fulfillment of our heart's desire, a dream, a passion, a goal. And while this is partially true since you need a north star to provide a clear direction for your energy, gifts, talents, skills, and ability—what you are actually committing to is to become the person you would be when your dream is fulfilled. Not to wait until your dream is fulfilled, but at the very moment you commit you are declaring your faith in your intention through your thoughts, beliefs, feelings, choices, words, and actions. You are actually living from the future of your dream achieved!

INSPIRED LIFE LIST:
DO WHAT YOU SAY YOU'RE GONNA DO

Explore your commitments to yourself by writing your responses to the following questions:

- ❀ What are your commitments to yourself?

- ❀ What commitment(s) have you been hesitant to make?

- ❀ What would you commit to if you knew you could not fail?

- ❀ What commitments do you make today to nourish your inspired life?

Gail Lynne Goodwin, the founder of inspiremetoday.com, knows the power of committing first. Here is her story:

I always felt that I lived an inspired, giving, and positive life. I was committed to playing bigger, using my talents, skills, and abilities to inspire others. I woke up one morning in 2004 and immediately called my daughter Carly, an aspiring recording artist, and told her, "I've got a song for you. I heard it in a dream last night."

She responded like any twenty-something daughter and said, "Mom, you're a real estate developer. You live in L.A., I live in Nashville. I hang out with really good song-writers. Thanks, but no thanks. Keep your day job!"

I said, "I didn't write this. You sang it to me all night long. You have to listen to it."

I flew to Nashville, and along with songwriter Gerald Smith, Carly and I co-wrote the song, "Baby Come Back Home," honoring the unrecognized, often unnoticed, sacrifices of soldiers' wives.

From the success of a simple audio postcard containing the song, released on the Internet, we accepted invitations, and during the next two years visited about a hundred military bases in the US, made three trips to Guantanamo Bay, and then spent twenty-nine days in Iraq and six countries in the Persian Gulf entertaining our troops and their families.

During a trip to Guantanamo Bay, Cuba, I was chal-

lenged by a Marine, who lamented that America had forgotten the troops. Inspired to prove him wrong, we set out on a trip across America gathering personal messages of love and support on newsprint scrolls. We amassed more than eighteen miles of messages on the Baby Come Back Home Soldier Scrolls.

Just after Congress signed the scrolls on the floor of the US Capitol building in Washington, D.C, we departed on a twenty-nine-day tour to Iraq and six other countries in the Persian Gulf, literally wrapping the love and support of America around each of the eighteen bases we visited on this musical tour.

After a concert at Al Qa'im, a remote base in Iraq, a young Marine named Jesse approached me with a simple request for a "mom hug." He said that he'd been off the base for thirty-seven days, hadn't had a shower, and asked if he could still have his hug. He'd just turned nineteen and hadn't been touched in nine months and four days. As I hugged him, wiping tears from my eyes, Jesse explained that his job required him to live in a ditch, alone for thirty to forty days at a time. More than eight hundred other Marines guard this stretch of desert and do the same thing, coming back to the base for only a few days every month or so. Jesse explained that he survives the solitude by listening to music on his iPod and shared that he's "always looking for good inspiration."

I had made a commitment to play big, not exactly sure

what that meant. Then, I had a dream, I heard a song and the words of W. H. Murray came to life, "A whole stream of events issues from the decision, raising in one's favor all manner of unforeseen incidents, meetings, and material assistance, which no man could have dreamt would have come his way."

Feeling like I'd been hit by lightning by Jesse's request for inspiration, I returned home and followed my dream, founding inspiremetoday.com in April of 2008.

SUPPORT YOUR COMMITMENTS

List commitments that are challenging for you to keep. Next to each item on your list, write the thoughts you'd have to think to support you in living your commitments. Share your list with a person you trust—a vision keeper buddy. Ask your vision keeper to remind you of these thoughts when you are feeling challenged in keeping your commitments.

GOD: GROUNDED IN A SPIRITUAL CENTER

We are all composed of the same matter even though things look different. When we dissect things down to their smallest components, everything—trees, flowers, grains of salt, rocks, insects, birds, fish, humans—is composed of the same waves of energy vibrating at different frequencies. Everything is energy. And energy is the basis of our spiritual connection and power.

—The Mind Manual System

There are many names for our spiritual source: God, Goddess, Buddha, Jesus, Allah, Loving Energy of the Universe, the Great Mystery, Spirit Guide, Inner Self, Higher Self, True Self, Greater Field of Life, Super Consciousness, etc... Regardless of the name, our spiritual power is an invisible force, abundant and present throughout the universe and is your co-creative partner and energetic source in living and evolving your inspired life.

To understand our spiritual nature more deeply, Peter Russell, author of *From Science to God: A Physicist's Journey into the Mystery of Consciousness*, writes:

The essence of spirituality is the search to know our true selves, to discover the real nature of consciousness. This quest has been the foundation of all the great spiritual teachings, and the goal of all the great mystics.

Throughout the history of humanity it has been said that the self we know—the individual ego—is a very limited form of identity. Ignorant of our true selves we derive a false sense of identity from what we have, or what we do—from our possessions, our role in the world, how others see us, etc. Because the world on which it is based is continually changing, this derived sense of identity is always under threat, and our attempts to maintain it are responsible for much of our "self-centered" behavior.

Behind this identity is a deeper identity, what is often called the "true self." This can be thought of as the essence of consciousness. Although our thoughts, feelings, and personality may vary considerably, the essence of mind remains the same. We are each very different people than we were twenty years ago, but still we feel the same sense of "I." This sense of "I-ness" is the same for everyone, and in that respect is something universal that we all share.

When we discover this deeper sense of self we are freed from many of the fears that plague us unnecessarily. We discover a greater inner peace, an inner security that does not depend upon events or circumstances in the world around us. As a result we become less self-centered, less needy of the other's approval or recognition, less needy of collecting possessions and social status, and become happier, healthier, and more loving people. In many spiritual teachings this is called "self-liberation."

Most spiritual teachings also maintain that when one comes to know the true nature of consciousness, one also comes to know God. If God is the essence of the whole of creation, then God is the essence of every creature, and every person. This is why the search to discover the nature of one's own innermost essence is the search for God.

Whatever your name for God may be and however you seek to strengthen that connection: through a walk in the woods, a Sunday church service, reading inspiring words, a 12-Step program meeting, a yoga class, singing, dancing, or going within to the silent sacred center of your being, it is this connection with source energy—the Greater Field of Life—that not only fuels but is your co-creative partner in living an inspired life.

Susyn consciously began her spiritual journey when she participated in a Silva Mind Control program in 1972. A friend of hers had extra tickets to a weekend workshop, and that was enough reason for Susyn and her then-husband to check it out. Her journey has continued:

In the spring of 2010 I participated in a ten-week Love Mastery Program led by Katherine Woodward Thomas and Claire Zammit. Each week we were asked to write responses to questions pertaining to the lessons covered that week. On May twelfth, in response to, "What shifts for you when you relate to God/Spirit/the Universe as a partner vs. a parent?" I wrote:

When I relate to God/Spirit/the Universe as a partner—as my co-creative partner—I understand in my mind and experience in my heart that limitless possibility is available to me. I come to know that in the center of my being, pulsing in every cell, I have a partner who meets my wishes, intent, and desire with a resounding "yes."

From this perspective, through my spiritual eyes and "I" it is my responsibility to create from the center of my true love identity—my true self. Having God/Spirit/the Universe as my co-creative partner means that creating from the center of my false love identity (my ego identity—my I'm-not-enough-ness) will generate the same resounding "yes" as creating from my true love identity. So I have a direct role in this creative process.

When I relate to God/Spirit/the Universe as my co-creative partner, I am empowered. If God is my partner, then I am equal to God in that I have an equal role to play in the creative process. From this point of view I see that the choices I make have value, have an impact, and do make a difference. If I want the world to be a more loving, peaceful place, then I am responsible in my thoughts, words, and actions to be a peacemaker—to be the world's greatest lover.

There is a prayer called the "Prayer for Protection," written by James Dillet Freeman, for all soldiers during World War II; it was carried by astronaut Col. James "Buzz" Aldrin on Apollo 11 on the very first flight to the moon:

The Light of God surrounds me.
The Love of God enfolds me.
The Power of God protects me.
The Presence of God watches over me.
The Mind of God guides me.
The Life of God flows through me.
The Laws of God direct me.
The Power of God abides within me.
The Joy of God uplifts me.
The Strength of God renews me.
The Beauty of God inspires me.
Wherever I am, God is!

When I first heard this prayer I thought the last line, "Wherever I am, God is," meant that if I crossed the street, then God would be there. Wherever I went God would be there. And even though this meaning offered me the opportunity to meet God wherever I went, this was the notion of a God outside of me, a man with a long white beard, not necessarily up in the sky, but separate from me with the power to judge my actions and grant or not grant my wishes.

I clearly remember the day when my understanding of this line of the prayer evolved and I "got" that, "wherever I am God is," means that God is always with me. This placed God within me, transforming my relationship to one of a co-creative partnership. In this partnership I set the course by committing to the vision that is revealed to me when I go within and listen to that still, small voice, the voice of my true self, of God. When I in-tend this vision, tend to it from the inside out, with faith and conviction, then my partner, the Greater Field of Love and Life, aligns with my energetic vibration, and to quote W. H. Murray, "raising in one's favor all manner of unforeseen incidents, meetings, and material assistance, which no man could have dreamt would have come his way."

INSPIRED LIFE ACTION: HAVE A CONVERSATION WITH GOD
Strengthen your connection with your spiritual center by having a conversation with God (or whatever name you are comfortable using to describe source energy). Write a letter to God, asking about your next step to fulfill your dreams, asking how to deepen your connection, asking how to differentiate between the wisdom of God and the

voice of your ego-mind, etc. For the last line of your letter, write, *Dear God, please write your response in a letter to me. Thank you.* And then, free of judgment, allow God to write to you, through your pen.

Remember: You always have access to Universal Source Energy. Your connection may simply have to be cultivated. Once it is, you are tapped into the most powerful co-creative partner around and this is the true source of breathing life into your inspired life vision.

DAILY SPIRITUAL PRACTICE

Create a daily spiritual practice. You may follow a specific structure every day: begin each morning with an inspirational reading, meditate for twenty minutes, and at the end of the day, write a gratitude list of five things you are grateful for. Or you may chant for fifteen minutes on Monday, Wednesday, and Friday; meditate on Tuesday, Thursday, and Saturday for twenty minutes; and write in your journal for fifteen minutes on Sunday. Approach your practice keeping in mind Marianne Williamson's words "The goal of spiritual practice is full recovery, and the only thing you need to recover from is a fractured sense of self. To go within is not to turn your back on the world; it is to prepare ourselves to serve it most effectively."

HEALING: FREE THE WOUNDS OF THE PAST

In relationships, as in the physical body, a thorn close to the surface may work itself out, but an internal infection buried deep and disregarded will threaten health and even life.

—Philip Yancey

A major tenet of living an inspired life is being awake and grounded in the present moment, as your greatest point of power. When your attention and energy is directed toward and drained by past circumstances that have caused you suffering, anger, hurt, resentment, and a desire for revenge, you do not have full access to your creative potential in the present moment. You are actually nourishing, reactivating, and reinforcing old wounds. You are being abusive to yourself based upon the meaning you are continuing to give to circumstances from your past.

Yes, it is true that in your past you may have experienced horrific physical and/or emotional abuse and disappointments. Long after the wounds of the physical abuse heal, the emotional wounds linger based on the beliefs—the meaning you have attached to the circumstances. Some of your wounds occurred when you were very young, so it appears that their meaning has been hardwired into your psyche.

I am reminded of a story I read in Caroline Myss's book, *Energy Anatomy*, many years ago. She writes about a woman, who as a six-year-old child, experienced incest during a twenty-minute period. Now, forty years later, this continued to be the defining experience of her life. She attended multiple incest survivors support groups each week. When asked, in present time, how she was feeling her response always began with a reference to something that had come up in one of her support groups and reactivated the wounds of her forty-year-old incest experience.

Freeing yourself from the wounds of your past is not about repressing past experiences, pretending they didn't occur, or wishing your past had been different. Rather, it is about letting go of the meaning you have attached to the circumstance and freeing both your heart and mind to be more fully awake to the present moment.

"Sure," you may be thinking, "Easy for you to say, but how do I do this?" The actions that allow you to complete the past are forgiveness and gratitude.

FORGIVENESS: FREEING YOUR HEART

When you hold resentment toward another, you are bound to that person or condition by an emotional link that is stronger than steel. Forgiveness is the only way to dissolve that link and get free.

—Catherine Ponder

Quite simply forgiveness is the act of pardoning or excusing oneself or someone else without harboring resentment. Keeping in mind that it is a real challenge for us to forgive someone for something we believe is absolutely wrong, it is then crucial to understand that forgiveness is not condoning hurtful or harmful behavior. It is freeing your heart and mind from the meaning you have made about yourself, others, and life, which were generated by the wounding circumstance and continue to cause you misery. We have found it very useful to remember that at each and every moment everyone—yes, everyone—is doing the very best they can, based on their thinking, their programming.

Most of us automatically operate from programming generated from our ego-mind which judges, separates, and defines circumstances in terms of "right" and "wrong," "good" and "bad." Forgiveness requires another point of view, that we see all life through our "spiritual eyes." It is through this perspective that we are aware that:

❀ We are One—while we look separate, as though there is space and distance between us, we are moving through the world breathing the very same air. Our thoughts, all of our thoughts, contribute to the universal collective consciousness of all beings. If we desire a more peaceful, joyful, and loving world, it is up to each of us to be the ones who are for giving—being the cheerleaders for—peace and love.

❀ Life is a Gift—offering us the opportunity to savor, enjoy, celebrate, and honor the mysterious human experience. To continually nourish misery and suffering in our lives, diminishes our capacity to truly see and receive the gifts life offers.

❀ Humans are Meaning-Making Machines— the meanings we give to the circumstances of our lives, based on our beliefs about ourselves, others, and life, are the source of our feelings, actions, and experiences.

While you may understand the concepts that define what it means to experience the world through your "spiritual eyes," in order for an inspired life to take root in your life, you must live from this point of view reflected in your thoughts, feelings, choices, words, and actions. When you notice and are aware that you are attached to resentments, the desire to be "right" or to seek revenge, this is the time to put forgiveness into action.

INSPIRED LIFE ACTION: FORGIVING YOURSELF

We are often asked, *"What is the most important way to initiate forgiveness in our lives?"* Our answer is always the same, *"Begin by forgiving yourself."*

- ❀ Make a list of things you want to forgive yourself for. Your list may include judgments you have about your body, your abilities, your behaviors, your addictions, and so on.

- ❀ When your list is completed, read it aloud by stating before each item in the list, *"I am ready and willing to forgive myself for _____ _____."*

- ❀ For items on the list you can readily let go of, cross them out.

❧ If you come to an item you feel hesitant about forgiving yourself for, ask yourself, *"What would it take to forgive myself for _____*

_____?"

❧ When you have crossed out all of the items on your list, burn the list and use the ashes as fertilizer in a plant or offer them up to be carried away on the wind as a reflection of the transformative power of forgiveness.

❧ Declare aloud, *"I am For Giving love, compassion, and kindness."*

Remember: Since some of the items on your list may have had a very long lifespan, it may take more than one sitting to complete the exercise. Do not judge yourself for the amount of time it takes!

Sheri Rosenthal, co-founder of www.withforgiveness.com, learned about the transformational power of forgiveness when she looked within her wounded mind and stopped blaming her mother for her past unhappiness. Here is her story:

Before I started on my spiritual path, I was quite challenged by the idea of forgiveness. I knew it was something that I should do, but more often than not I was too angry at the person involved to forgive them. Even when I thought I had forgiven someone, all they had to do was to be around me again, and sure enough, I would be seething. I did not get how forgiveness was supposed to make me feel better, nor could I figure out what it was that I was supposed to "let go" of.

I came to understand that the problem was my wounded mind, not the doings of others. I realized people did and said all kinds of things I might not agree with or I judged to be wrong. But so what? I was never going to change that—the only thing I could change was the way I chose to perceive and interpret what they were doing and saying. This understanding opened the possibility of transforming my relationship with my mother.

My whole life I have loved my mom dearly, however, our relationship was difficult and tumultuous. We screamed at, hurt, and judged one another. After ten minutes of being together, we would find something to bicker or argue about. I always thought that if she went to therapy, everything would be fine, since she was the problem (from my point of view, of course!).

As I began my spiritual path, I started looking at my childhood and life, seeking to better understand myself and why I was never truly happy. I realized I blamed my mom for my childhood and all the "terrible" injustices I suffered. I saw my childhood as painful, shameful, and horrible. As a result I was subconsciously punishing my mom for all the suffering she caused me. I wanted her to pay—and she paid dearly every day of her life, believe me!

Meanwhile, my anger toward my mom had her feeling so guilty she had no choice but to defend herself in my presence, to protect herself against all the guilt I was trying to make her feel. In return, she projected her anger at me. It was a vicious cycle.

Then one day I was hiking along the north rim of the Grand Canyon and I heard a voice in my head that said, "You must let go of all the anguish and grief about your childhood." For a second, I thought, "I don't have any anguish and grief." But lo and behold, a flood of emotion rushed out of me as I sat on the canyon rim, all the stored-up anger I felt toward my mom. And then it was gone. When I stood up, I was exhausted, but I knew I was done. I was no longer angry at my mom. I felt the most intense wave of love and compassion for her.

What had changed in that moment? I realized my childhood was no different from any other person who grew up in a dysfunctional home. I recognized my inner child was angry for not receiving the unconditional love she felt she needed. I had been focusing on only what was terrible in my life and I made the unconscious choice, as a child, to see my mom as a tyrant. I finally saw the truth of the situation: my mom loved me and she was doing the best she could.

That evening as I was soaking in the bath, my mom phoned me quite upset. She felt like something significant had changed between us that day. Amazingly, my mom actually perceived the dissolution of the entire energetic prison that had us chained together in a constant cycle of emotional pain!

I told her that earlier in the day, I had let go of all the anger I had felt toward her and that I loved and appreciated her. I said I was sorry for being so mean and for constantly trying to punish her when she was doing her best. I had forgiven her.

After this experience forgiveness became easy for me. I finally understood that I needed to let go of the way I chose to see the world. I saw that life is what it is. You can be angry about things and blame others, or you can understand why people behave the way they do and let it go. Just so you know, my mom and I have never argued once since that day and she is my best friend.

Taking responsibility for the way I perceived and interpreted reality and then how I reacted emotionally was critical to my freedom. The key to my peace and happiness was in healing my own mind with truth, forgiveness, and love.

WHAT YOU THINK ABOUT FORGIVENESS

Write your thoughts about forgiveness. What does it mean to you? What blocks you from being forgiving? What do Jesus's words from the cross mean to you: "Forgive them, for they know not what they do"? How can you use his lesson in your life? What have you learned by focusing your attention on forgiveness?

GRATITUDE: LIVING YOUR LIFE AS A THANK YOU

Gratefulness is the key to a happy life that we hold in our hands, because if we are not grateful, then no matter how much we have we will not be happy, because we will always want to have something else or something more.

—Brother David Steindl-Rast

When you acknowledge what is right in your life, you experience greater joy, happiness, confidence, and fulfillment, which are crucial elements for living a joyous, inspired life. You trust your ability and that support, visible and invisible, is available to you to successfully meet and navigate life's challenges.

Problems do not seem as overwhelming when you take a few moments to count your blessings and appreciate what exists in your life. Emotionally, gratitude is the equivalent of taking a deep breath and relaxing.

Research shows that people who actively practice appreciation and gratitude in their lives are happier. The expression of gratitude is a feeling, a sense of awe, wonder, and appreciation for what you have and what is around you.

Plato said more than 2500 years ago, "A grate-
ful mind is a great mind which eventually attracts
to itself great things." A tremendous insight! The
grateful person is great because he or she has
turned on all the lights within. You may say of
someone, "He has so much, and he is so grate-
ful." But by Plato's law, it may be that he has so
much because he is so grateful. The grateful heart
actually opens the way to the flow and becomes an
attractive force to draw to itself great things.

—Eric Butterworth

Recognizing what is beautiful and good in your life trains your mind to think in positive and fulfilling ways. An attitude of gratitude brings peace of mind and contentment to the present moment, and anxiety and fear dissipate because you are actively strengthening an empowered brain pathway.

As with forgiveness, you may know that this is a good idea, but until you put an attitude of gratitude into practice in your life you do not reap the benefits it offers.

There are two major challenges to navigate in order to have ready access to gratitude. The first is when you are automatically used to seeing what is wrong or lacking in any situation, no matter what the circumstance. A simple example of this is when your boss compliments you for a job well done and instead of being grateful and allowing yourself to receive the recognition you find something wrong with the way it was given or the timing. "I always do a good job, why didn't she tell me in person, rather than in an email?" or "Why did she have to wait so long to tell me? I bet she just wants to dump another project on me." Or, a friend comments on how good your new haircut looks and, again, instead of simply saying, "Thanks for the compliment," you point out all the reasons you don't like the haircut. In these examples your inability to graciously receive and be grateful for the recognition you are getting keeps you piling up evidence that squelches living an inspired life.

To counteract this habit of thinking, you must remember that when you receive a compliment, the most valuable response you can offer is to say, "Thank you!" and allow this acknowledgment to actually touch you and fill your heart. Initially this will not be your automatic reaction but over time you will create a new brain pathway allowing you to live life as a "thank you."

The second challenge to experiencing gratitude is the difficulty of seeing the gift hidden within a disappointment, loss, or sense of betrayal. Katherine Woodward Thomas, best-selling author of *Calling in "The One"* and co-founder of the Feminine Power Global Community, describes in her essay, "The Beauty of the Dark Night," how it took her years to uncover the gift in the nightmare her life became when she was nineteen years old.

For a time after high school, I was totally uninterested in going to college. My burning passion was to become a missionary serving God by serving others. Instead of heading off to university, then, I went straight into Bible School, filled with a sense of noble purpose and resolve to make something beautiful of my life. During the year I was there, I spent much of my time alone in the chapel in deep contemplation and prayer.

Sometimes I would kneel at the altar for hours, literally begging God to use my life in service to something meaningful and deeply good. I expected therefore, that I would soon be offered opportunities to give my gifts to the world in inspiring and exciting ways. What happened instead was nothing short of a nightmare. Complete devastation!

My boyfriend of several years up and married someone else, my best friend turned against me and took with her our entire community of friends, and the eating disorder I'd had since I was fourteen years old took over my life with a vengeance, adding fifty pounds to my rather petite frame within a matter of months. I was estranged from my parents, having gone against their wishes for me to attend college with a fierce and righteous defiance. I had absolutely nowhere to turn and no one to go to, plummeting into an isolated stupor.

One might hope that a person of faith would turn toward God in a time of deep despair, yet what I did instead was turn away. I was furious, feeling betrayed on the deepest level by a God who clearly couldn't care less about me, and my idealistic, naive prayers. I stopped praying altogether, and began a long, dark journey that would last for years.

I humbly returned home to attend classes at a local community college, before transferring to a proper university the following year. Although I'd been a social person all through high school, I spent the majority of my college years isolated and alone, without any friends to speak of.

My early twenties improved somewhat when I moved to New York City and discovered a passion for acting and singing. Yet I was still deeply lost and confused, and still a good deal overweight. It was during this period that I began therapy and participating in the very empowering transformative seminar, Lifespring.

I also found my way into a 12 Step Program for food addicts. I identified greatly with the others in the "rooms" but I had a huge dilemma. I hadn't prayed in years. Six to be exact! And since the 12 Step Program is a spiritual program, I faced a breakdown, for sure. I spent the first few weeks of that program figuring out how to deal with this challenge until I finally surrendered and realized there was no way around it. I would have to pray again. That night I got down on my knees and prayed a rather unorthodox, if not downright irreverent prayer. "F*@k you, God," I said. At least it got us talking again!

I spent the next twelve years in the program. It was

an intense time where I pretty much worked on myself full-time. One of those years I even went to three meetings a day— morning, noon, and night—because I was so nonfunctional. Yet all of that effort paid off because by the time I was in my mid-thirties, I had pretty much resolved the eating disorder and had recovered enough to consider myself a relatively well and sane person.

I was deeply grateful. To celebrate, I made an offering to God. I would do something beautiful for the community. But what to do? I began praying, "God, what can I do to express my thanks? What offering can I make to show you my gratitude?" For six weeks I prayed, asking and listening, and then it came to me clear as a bell.

I was a singer and songwriter; I knew the healing and regenerative power of music. The clear flash of inspiration I received was to go down to Skid Row and work with people who were homeless. I was to give them a voice by making a CD of music and lyrics they would write in collaboration with professional songwriters. So I started a project called "In Harmony with the Homeless."

Now I didn't know anything about how to do this. I'd never made a CD before, and I'd never led a creative writing workshop before. But that was the directive and I'm very obedient!

So I went down to one of the missions where people went to recover from drug and alcohol addiction and to rehabilitate their lives. As a first step, I gathered eighteen people who'd been sober for six months and I started a series of creative writing workshops. These men and women would get together each weekend to share and write about all they'd learned in those six months, solidifying their gains and evolving their stories into hopeful tributes to the love of God and the power of the human spirit. The changes they were experiencing were phenomenal, and it became evident that the workshops themselves were having a magical effect upon their lives. They were having life-altering experiences—their lives were literally transforming inside of the program I'd created.

During one of our meetings I had a sudden epiphany. I thought of the nightmare my life had become when I was nineteen years old, and how fiercely I'd believed that God had abandoned and betrayed me. Yet, in this moment, I could see that it wasn't like that at all. Rather, I suddenly realized that the plunge into darkness and the subsequent years of recovery work I'd had to do to climb out were actually the answer to my prayers. It was inside of those experiences that I now knew exactly what to do to help others find their way, too. As a matter of fact, just who I was seemed to lift people up, as though I held a transmission of sorts, embodying the very sense of possibility I was eager to impart.

So now, whenever I walk through a dark time, I try to remember to have faith, particularly in the face of no evidence. For everything we go through, even the biggest disappointments and failures, gives us the opportunity, offers us the gift, to make something beautiful of our lives.

(Note: Katherine Woodward Thomas has helped tens of thousands of people overcome adversity and find their way toward creating happy, healthy, and meaningful lives.)

INSPIRED LIFE PRACTICE:
CREATE A GRATITUDE LIST WITH NEW THINGS EVERY DAY
For thirty consecutive days make a list of at least five things you are grateful for. Include on each list one item you have never before expressed gratitude for (dental floss, your toenails), as well as one item that is a gift, which was hidden in a challenge, problem, or disappointment (the gift of a traffic jam may be patience, the gift of disagreement may be learning to accept another point of view, etc.). Be creative.

Remember: The more you practice gratitude, the faster it becomes your dominant habitual pattern of thinking, and the more consciously and actively you are deepening and expanding your capacity for joy.

HOW MANY TIMES CAN YOU SAY "THANK YOU"?

Express your gratitude throughout the day by saying, "thank you." Set a challenge for yourself: *today I am going to say "thank you" fifty times, one hundred times, or even more.* You may say "thank you" to the person in the car in front of you, who is driving slowly, for giving you an opportunity to practice patience!

A CLEAR NORTH STAR IS YOUR PERSONAL GPS

An inspired life is living deeply connected with the divine, invisible force of life and love. From this powerful connection, we make choices that honor us fully and thereby honor others as well. There's an ease. There's a knowing that we are in alignment with our greatest purpose for being here. Miracles happen because our eyes are open to seeing them. Challenges become opportunities to evolve. Every moment carries the possibility for experiencing great joy.

—*Lyndra Hearn Antonson*

A north star provides direction. Have you ever looked up at the sky on a dark, clear night catching sight of that one bright star, the North Star? And whether or not you know very much about the location of the constellations or the planets, there is something familiar and even inspiring in this recognition.

The same is true for each of us. In our lives having a north star, a clear vision and a sense of purpose providing direction for our life and articulating our dreams, is a mandatory ingredient for living an inspired life.

Defining your north star requires your willingness to ask and answer the following questions:

- ❀ What is my heart's desire?

- ❀ What is my life's purpose?

- ❀ What are my greatest gifts, talents, abilities, and skills?

These questions are not answered by what you think you *should* do. What your parents want you to do. What other people are doing. Or even what seems practical, reasonable, and logical for you to do. These questions are answered when you have the courage to go within and ask the questions and listen to the answers. You may be wondering, *why do I need courage to do this?* You need courage because you may not get the answer you expect, and you must be willing to allow the full range of possibilities to emerge.

Susyn describes how it was courage that allowed her to face her fears and for her north star to be revealed. Here is her story:

In early 2002, I was, yet again, at a crossroads in my life. I was hungry for a clear direction. My life was actually quite appealing if you looked at it from the outside. I was single again, and with this freedom my choices were all up to me. But having limitless possibility can be as scary as having a sense of limited possibility! I lived in a beautiful home on the eastern end of Long Island. I took long morning walks on the beach with my dog. My organization development consulting practice was lucrative. I was a grandmother for the first time. My life was filled with family, friends, and travel. I was healthy. But I wasn't feeling inspired. I wasn't feeling a zest for life.

So one morning I decided to have a conversation with God. Sitting on my bed, my journal on my lap, and my favorite pen in hand, I wrote, "Dear God, What is my next chapter in living an inspired life?" After writing this question, I was stopped in my tracks. I became anxious and afraid. What if I didn't like the answer? What if I was doomed to being single forever and each day was simply a repeat of the day before? What if I was too old for another chapter of inspiration in my life? I saw an image of me clutching with claw-like fingernails onto the side of a very tall mountain peak—Mount Fear—I was holding on for dear life.

Then my courage kicked in. I remembered, I believe in a Loving God. I believe that inspired possibility is alive in each and every moment—independent of age, gender, marital status, and history. I took a deep breath, closed my eyes, and said aloud, "Okay God, what is my next *chapter in living an inspired life?" And I saw the most wonderful vision unfold before me. My North Star was shining brightly once again.*

An inspired life is to be awestruck by the beauty of sunlight on the leaves, to cherish equally the cries and gurgles of babies and to remember your dreams every day.

—Lynn E. Geiger

PURPOSE: LIVING YOUR VALUES

The way you get meaning into your life is to devote yourself to loving others, devote yourself to your community around you, and devote yourself to creating something that gives you purpose and meaning.

—Mitch Albom

Becoming clear about the purpose for your life is not about having a list of specific action steps—that comes later—rather, it is knowing what the north star of your life is. To live an inspired life your purpose must be grounded in your values (integrity, walking your talk, being of service, continually evolving your capacity to give and receive love, etc.) and the specific gifts, talents, abilities, and skills you have to offer.

When you focus on your purpose you experience a resounding *yes*, in every cell of your being. While your purpose is reflected in what you do, and this may take many different forms in one lifetime, it starts with being aligned with who you are. Your purpose is your *raison d'être*, and while you may not be sure how to bring your purpose to life, simply having clarity about what it is miraculously generates opportunities to live your life on purpose.

David Riklan, founder of selfgrowth.com, turned his search for his purpose into a thriving portal for self-development information and resources. Here is David's story:

I'd been struggling with the concept of "what's my life's purpose?" Life purpose is one of those big, big things: "Why are we here? What's our purpose in life, what is the meaning of life?" This struggle began when I was a teenager and continued into my early twenties, trying to figure out, What's my purpose? What am I about? What am I here for? It was a big challenge for me.

I remember in high school and college there were a lot of people I knew, a lot of friends and acquaintances, who already had a vision for their lives. They knew they were going to be a successful attorney; they knew they were going to go to medical school and become a doctor or an orthopedic surgeon. They knew what they wanted to do and they were inspired and driven by their clarity of purpose. I was definitely not one of them. I didn't know what my purpose was, but I sure wanted one!

I set myself on a path. I said, "I'm going to figure this out. This is something I really want to know. I want to know what my life purpose is." I asked myself, "What's the best way to figure out what my life purpose is?" It seemed to me that in order to have the clarity I desired I'd need to know more. I'd need to be a better person, to be smarter, and to be more inspired and better at everything I did.

So I started on this path of what I can best describe as self-improvement. I started learning about how to improve my life. I was taking courses from Dale Carnegie and listening to tapes and CDs—actually it was pre-CDs—from Tony Robbins and Zig Ziglar.

While on this path of self-improvement I was growing and things started to gel. I suddenly had this epiphany that even though I didn't know right now what my life purpose is, I decided that my life's purpose was going to be to find out what my life's purpose is! I made finding out my life's purpose, my life's purpose. For me the best way to do this was to continue to learn and grow.

So the question then became, "If I continue to learn, improve, and grow, how do I turn this into a vocation? How do I turn this into making a living?" I decided one of the best ways to do this was to put myself into a position where I could help others learn as well. And this was the birth of www.selfgrowth.com.

Through selfgrowth.com I was able to accomplish two things at the same time: to continually research and find new methodologies and systems to improve my life and offer this information to others so they can discover how to improve their lives and to figure out what their life's purposes are. So through my quest to uncover my life's purpose, I'm helping other people find theirs.

A primary thing that drives me and nourishes my inspired life on a daily basis is my knowledge that I'm helping folks. Every day via emails and posts on our website, we hear from people saying, "Thanks for this great information" or "I'm so inspired by you and what you're doing."

Every time I know I'm helping folks, I'm inspired to do even more. In my mind, I'm just a fraction of the way there. You know, we're getting a million people coming to the website every month right now and I think I'm at one percent of where I need to be. Knowing I'm at one percent means I have another ninety-nine percent to go. This inspires me to continue providing more information, to a larger audience, and to help more people improve their lives, bringing me closer to living my life's purpose.

INSPIRED LIFE LIST: DEFINE YOUR PURPOSE

Answer the questions:

- ❀ What is my heart's desire?

- ❀ What is my life's purpose?

- ❀ What are my greatest gifts, talents, abilities, and skills?

We have found that some of our clients are able to answer these questions immediately, while others require time—days, weeks, months, and sometimes longer—for this inquiry. This is not a competition. You will know when you have identified *your* purpose when you experience a combination of a quiet knowing, and an inspired, resounding *yes* filling every cell of your being.

Remember: Too often we dismiss our true purpose, because we are fearful that we don't know what to do, how to live it, or it seems too lofty or bigger than we are. That is the thing about our purpose, it is our big dream; it does require that we see beyond the definitions of our personality—our ego selves—and that we acknowledge ourselves as co-creative partners with the Greater Field of Life. When you are grounded in your commitment to living your life on purpose, to living an inspired life, you invite and allow the resources of the universe to be your partner, on an as-needed basis, as in the movie, *Indiana Jones and The Temple of Doom,* the bridge appears with each step Indiana Jones takes across the chasm.

> *An inspired life is filled with intentional, passionate creation and grateful, graceful acceptance.*
> —Diana Daffner

VISION: CREATING THE LIFE YOU WANT

Formulate and stamp indelibly on your mind a mental picture of yourself succeeding. Hold this picture tenaciously. Your mind will seek to develop this picture.

—Norman Vincent Peale

While your purpose is an idea, your vision is a picture of that idea. Remembering that everything that exists in our physical reality begins in your mind as a dream, an idea, a concept—whether it is a paper clip, a new product, a relationship, war, peace, living an inspired life—it is necessary to create a mental picture which is a reflection of your purpose. This picture, your internal vision, provides the blueprint for your inspired life.

Since research has shown the brain does not distinguish between what is real in physical reality and what is imaginary, creating a vision of your purpose, of your inspired life, focusing your conscious attention on it, and naturally generating feelings and actions based on it is an expression of the creative process in action.

You may have heard about the power of having a clear vision described by John Assaraf, one of the experts featured in the best-selling book and film, *The Secret*. He had made a vision board collage that reflected his dreams for his life. As the years went by his vision board was packed away in his belongings. Many years after making his vision board he and his family moved into a new house. As he was unpacking, one of his children came across his vision board and asked him about it. As he looked at it and told his child about it, his eyes were drawn to the picture of the house he had pasted on his poster board collage many, many years earlier. He was startled when he realized he and his family were now living in that exact house. This is the power of having a clear vision.

Accessing the infinite resources of your imagination to visualize your dreams fulfilled and actually feeling the feelings of your desired result accomplished creates a potent impression on your brain, and a clear instruction to your co-creative partner, the Greater Field of Life, to provide and reveal the resources, opportunities, and next steps leading to improved performance and success. You react to the thoughts you think—your beliefs—which in turn create your feelings—the energetic vibrations that power the co-creative process.

A waitress who says, "How about a slice of our mouth-watering famous warm apple pie with a scoop of our creamy homemade vanilla bean ice cream and a dollop of freshly made delicious whipped cream?" is painting a word picture engaging your imagination and senses, and has a better chance of getting the dessert order than a waitress who simply says, "How about dessert?"

CREATE A VISION BOARD COLLAGE

With your purpose in mind create a collage of images and words that is a clear visual reflection of your inspired life. You may do this in one sitting, or gather the images in a folder and when you are ready, make your collage. As you choose your images and words, be guided by what "feels" right to you and be sure to include a picture of yourself. When your vision board collage is completed, place it somewhere where you can see it and "step into it," embodying the feelings of your vision fully achieved.

Remember: Thoughts generate feelings and always precede action. Visioning brings your thoughts and feelings to life from the inside out and inspires action. This process operates whether or not you are conscious of your thoughts, and whether or not your thoughts are focused on what you desire or fear. This is the creative process: Thoughts charged with emotional energy, spoken of with authority (you are the author), and acted on with conviction (faith).

VISUALIZE DESIRED OUTCOMES
THROUGHOUT THE DAY

Throughout the day see every situation you are about to step into as fully and completely satisfying. As you are getting out of bed in the morning, see yourself stepping out of the shower feeling refreshed, alert, clean, and eager for a fulfilling day. As you get ready to leave your house in the morning, see yourself safely arriving at your destination having enjoyed the journey. Play with this, have fun, and enjoy your day.

ACCEPTING "WHAT IS" AND FOCUSING ON WHAT YOU WANT

Transported to a surreal landscape, a young girl kills the first woman she meets and then teams up with three complete strangers to kill again.

—TV Listing for The Wizard of Oz

In order to understand the power of accepting "what is," it is necessary to distinguish between "what is" and drama. We were children in the 1950s when television was a new invention for sharing stories, a practice that began long, long, long ago around a hearth. A television was a prized possession, occupying center stage in the living room. While newspapers (there were many more of them then) and radio (there were fewer stations then) were available to report current events, having a real, live person seemingly join us in our living room was miraculous. Newscasters had an aura surrounding them as the purveyors of important facts—truth itself.

How times have changed! Now more than sixty years later, it is often difficult to distinguish new stories from entertainment, and reality TV from the drama of TV news. News pundits yell and denounce one another for voicing different points of view. With a twenty-four-hour news cycle on radio, TV, and the Internet, stories of terrorism, violence, and scandals are repeated, ensuring that images sustaining fear of the "enemy" are imprinted in our consciousness.

The word *television* can be heard as "tell-a-vision." In a thirty-second sound bite we are given a view of reality filled with commentary, judgments, and a skewed point of view. Confusion occurs when we do not understand the difference between "what is" and drama. The "what is" of any circumstance can be viewed as what has happened without all the judgments, points of view, and assumptions—"Just the facts, Jack." Drama occurs when we add judgments and opinions to the events and suffer the emotional turmoil that results. More often than not, these judgments are filled with blame and fuel the problem being reported, rather than directing us to focus our attention on the desired result and the steps to achieve an effective solution.

The same is true in our personal lives. We have the choice of describing "what is" when faced with a challenging circumstance, or offering the dramatic rendering. While the dramatic telling of your story may sound more interesting, more often than not this expression fuels judgments, assumptions, misery, and suffering. In turn, you then use the drama as evidence that life equals misery. And the more evidence you accumulate for this point of view, the more you believe it is the only point of view—that this is the truth.

Here are two examples which differentiate between drama and "what is":

Drama: A coaching client shared her story of how her husband recently had an affair. She related, "He betrayed me and made me feel like I caused our marital problems—in fact, he said it was because of me that he had an affair! Everyone in our community knew about his affair except for me. I was so humiliated. His girlfriend is about ten years younger than me and I feel so old and undesirable. I just want to find some way to make her miserable and suffer like I have."

What Is: My husband had a relationship outside of our marriage.

Drama: Another coaching client told me he had been overlooked for a promotion at work. He was furious because he had given his all to this job and now the person he had trained was promoted and is going to be his new boss. He said, "I'm ready to go to the VP of the department and read her the riot act. I can't believe I was betrayed, by the very person I trained!" As he continued to talk the fury was oozing from him as he listed the unjust and unfair policies of his company.

What Is: I did not get the promotion I wanted.

Living an inspired life means that you focus on "what is," free of the judgments of "right" or "wrong" or "good" or "bad," knowing there are gifts, although they may be hidden, in all circumstances, and all experiences have "come to pass," not to stay. Life is continually evolving, and what may seem like a tragedy in one moment may be exactly what was needed to direct you toward the fulfillment of your inspired life vision in the next.

The following teaching story, attributed to both the Sufis and Taoists, illustrates the wisdom of accepting "what is":

Once there was a farmer whose only possession was a prized horse. All the people of the village ridiculed him. "Why put all your money into a horse? Somebody could steal it and you will have nothing."

The horse did not get stolen, but sadly enough the horse did run away.

"You fool," the villagers said, "you should have diversified, not put so many eggs in one basket. Now you have nothing. You are so unlucky."

The farmer, being a wise man, answered, "Don't say I am unlucky. Just say my horse is no longer here. That is a fact. We don't know what may happen next."

Sure enough, the next day the horse returned, and with him was a herd of wild stallions. The villagers exclaimed, "You were so right. Look how fortunate you are!" The farmer replied, "You cannot possibly know if this is fortu-

nate or unfortunate. We do not have the whole story yet. Merely say that we have now more horses than before."

The farmer sent his only son to tame the wild horses. He was thrown and broke his leg. The doctor said the farmer's son would be crippled for life. The villagers again decried his misfortune, but again the farmer asked them to withhold judgment.

Soon thereafter, a war broke out in their country and all the healthy young sons were drafted into battle. Only the farmer's son was left behind. The fighting was fierce and most of the other boys in the village died at war.

"You were right again, farmer," the villagers said. The farmer shouted, "On and on you go, judging this, judging that. Who do you think you are? How is it that you presume to know how this is all going to turn out?"

INSPIRED LIFE PRACTICE: ACCEPTING "WHAT IS"

For one week, practice accepting "what is," when you are talking about the situations in your life, whether they appear to be fortunes or misfortunes. Simply describe them as "what is" without attributing blame or "good" or "bad" meanings. Notice if your tendency is to automatically focus on drama, and what your experience is when you stick to "the facts, Jack."

Remember: As meaning-making machines humans have a tendency to automatically tell stories which reflect their beliefs about themselves, their relationships, and life. Notice what beliefs are being expressed through your stories.

An inspired life is enjoying and appreciating the journey, whatever it looks like.

—Maya Baker

WALK YOUR TALK: INSPIRATION INTO ACTION

When you pray, move your feet.

—*African Proverb*

As I researched the number of thoughts people have each day, there was not one definitive answer; rather, the range was between 60,000–86,400 thoughts per day. Whatever the exact number of daily thoughts we think, it's a lot of thoughts, each and every day. And, when you are not engulfed in thoughts which generate fear, hopelessness, anxiety, and worry about what you don't want or what you wish were different, there are probably thoughts, ideas, dreams, and goals which are the seeds of inspired living.

While we, and others throughout history, have written extensively that it is your thoughts, beliefs, assumptions, and choices which are the chief ingredients of the creative process, thoughts without action do not nurture and sustain an inspired life. Rather, it is your thoughts, aligned with your north star, generating your feelings (your magnetic vibrational frequency), and reflected in your actions that is the magic formula for a life of purpose, happiness, vitality, joy, and unprecedented love.

The way to get started is to quit talking and begin doing.

—Walt Disney

The message here is actually quite simple—to live an inspired life you must take action—in consciously choosing your thoughts and behaviors that are birthed from your personal inspired life vision. The first action required is to answer the question, "What is *my* vision of an inspired life?"

Remember: This is not what you think your vision should be, or what other people tell you it ought to be— this is your vision birthed from your inner knowing, which may start as a whisper, and pops into your mind over and over and over again, possibly through decades.

LIVING IN ALIGNMENT
(NO MATTER WHAT!)

AUTOBIOGRAPHY IN FIVE SHORT CHAPTERS
by Portia Nelson

I
I walk down the street.
There is a deep hole in the sidewalk.
I fall in.
I am lost...I am helpless.
It isn't my fault.
It takes me forever to find a way out.

II
I walk down the same street.
There is a deep hole in the sidewalk.
I pretend I don't see it.
I fall in again.
I can't believe I am in the same place,
but it isn't my fault.
It still takes a long time to get out.

III

I walk down the same street.
There is a deep hole in the sidewalk.
I see it is there.
I still fall in...it's a habit.
My eyes are open.
I know where I am.
It is my fault.
I get out immediately.

IV

I walk down the same street.
There is a deep hole in the sidewalk.
I walk around it.

V

I walk down another street.

While there may be an enormous gulf between your current reality and the life of your dreams, for your inspired life to take root you must live from the future of your vision fulfilled. Living in alignment with your inspired life vision can be described as living "as if." You are living "as if" your vision is fulfilled, with faith and conviction in your ability as a co-creative partner with the Greater Field of Life to achieve the results you desire, to out-picture your vision. This doesn't mean you will always follow a straight path in accomplishing your goals. It does mean that when obstacles appear, you take action based upon what you want to accomplish—not just based on eliminating the obstacle. Eve Eliot, a master meditation teacher says, *"Do not make decisions and take actions based on the avoidance of suffering."*

All too often people give up on their dreams, in the face of challenges to free themselves of the discomfort which arises when stopped in their tracks by a pothole smack dab in the center of their path. In *The Path of Least Resistance*, Robert Fritz writes about structural tension. This is the tension that is naturally present when there is a discrepancy between where you are and where you want to be. The danger to inspired living occurs when rather than seeing this tension as natural in the creative process, you experience it as psychological tension—worry, anxiety, hopelessness, fear—and then quickly take actions based solely on relieving your tension—which is a very different perspective than initiating actions congruent with your vision.

When faced with this tension, the effective actions include identifying "what is," acknowledging what you are feeling, reconnecting with your vision, and going within and asking, "In the presence of this challenge, what is the next step in my thinking, choices, and actions to continue to nourish my vision and allow support?" The difficult part for many of us, at this point, is that it may take some time to get clear about our next action step, and our impatience may get the upper hand leading us, all too often, to give up on our dreams, by using the obstacles as proof that "the universe doesn't want this for me." Allowing yourself time to "feel" your connection with your vision is not the same as giving up on it.

Remember: The universe is not a puppet master pulling your strings. The universe is the resounding *yes* of your co-creative partner responding to your dominant vibrational frequency—your dominant thoughts.

We have found that sometimes the best action to take is to meditate, spend time in nature, and connect with people who love you and have faith in your ability to be successful. Use your connection with your personal cheerleaders and their belief in you as a bridge to reconnecting with your passion, vitality, and inspiration.

When faced with a boulder in the road, Susyn was stopped in her tracks and used this time to rediscover her north star. Here is her story:

By June 2007, I had spent two-and-a-half amazing years, traveling and writing. During that time I had lived in San Francisco and outside of Sedona, Arizona. I'd traveled to Mexico, England, France, Italy, New Zealand, and Australia—and all through the United States. I had written my second book, The Gift of the Acorn, *and coauthored another,* WITH Forgiveness ~ Are You Ready? *I had been a delegate to the United Nations Commission on the Status of Women. They had been glorious years but I was feeling itchy to settle down, to get back to the East Coast.*

One night I opened an email and read about a job opening for a Program Director at Omega Institute in Rhinebeck, New York. In a flash, I knew this was the job for me, which was quite surprising since I had been self-employed for twenty-seven years!

The application process involved submitting an essay describing my qualifications and why I was the perfect applicant. It was due the next day! The next day I sat at my computer and my essay flowed effortlessly from my fingertips to my computer screen. I was pleased with what I wrote and was very excited that the next chapter of my life was before me. I would have the opportunity through this position at Omega to use my skills, contacts, and passion for personal growth and development to offer others opportunities to tap into their inspiration. In addition, I would be part of a community of like-minded people and I would be back on the East Coast. YAY!

After I clicked send on my computer to submit my application, within thirty minutes of the deadline, I emailed my family and friends, asking them to "see me in the job." I was so aligned with this goal, I could taste it...every cell in my being harmonized a resounding "yes." In the weeks and months to come my reality reflected my desire. There had been over three hundred applicants. I made the first cut; the next step, a phone conversation with the CEO, was scheduled. I passed through that hoop. The field was now down to ten and I was scheduled to go to Omega and meet with the Executive Staff.

I arrived in Rhinebeck early that day, and drove around town. Ah! This would be the perfect place for me to live. I got to Omega, quite a different place than when I had gone to a workshop during its very first season, at a school rented for the summer, and slept in a tent out in a field! The interview went well. I liked the people I met.

Then the days turned into weeks. I got an email to let me know a decision would soon be made. Humm, I wondered, "Would we keep the house in Arizona, how much time would I have before the job began?"

And then I got an email—it was the most beautiful rejection letter I had ever received—filled with feedback describing me in glowing terms and a clear explanation that the two finalists had extensive experience working in organizations that offered personal development programming, clearly not the jobs I had listed on my resume.

I was stopped in my tracks. I knew I had done my best. I had no regrets or "if onlys" crowding my thinking. But I became tense, with the uncertainty of what to do with my life. This job seemed to have been the answer to so many of my desires but it was not to be. I spent a few days lost in the enormity of having to, once again, "dream up" what was next for me.

And here is what happened: Within days I was invited to facilitate leadership development training programs in Arizona. I did that for the next year; during that year, I took the time to explore, from the inside out, "What is the next chapter of my inspired life?"

And now I am living it. I am back on the East Coast. Joan and I created self-esteem-experts.com and I am living my dream of working with people to expand and deepen their capacity to give and receive love—starting with loving themselves as the foundation of living an inspired life.

When I was met with a "no" in my professional life, rather than using this as evidence that life doesn't work for me, I reconnected with my inspired life vision. Maybe it's time for me to submit a workshop proposal to Omega!

INSPIRED LIFE LIST:
RECONNECT WITH YOUR VISION

Use the following steps when you are stopped in your tracks and lose connection with your inspired life vision:

❀ Acknowledge what you are feeling.

❀ Ask yourself, "What do I need to do right now to reconnect with my vision?"

❀ Take action to align with your vision.

❀ When you are reconnected with your vision, ask yourself, "What is my next step which reflects the fulfillment of my dreams?"

❀ Take action.

Remember: The fulfillment of your vision may not always look like what you think it should. Your work, where you focus your energy and attention, is to continue to stay connected with your inspired life vision and take action "as if" success is a given.

ENLIST THE SUPPORT
OF A VISION KEEPER

When you have fallen into a pothole of fear and hopeless-ness on the path to living your inspired life vision, it often feels much too difficult to find your way out. This is the time to reach out to a personal cheerleader, your vision keeper. Call a friend, family member, mentor, or coach who has faith in your ability to succeed and ask for their help, which may include listening as you vent, reminding you that you are capable, suggesting your next step. Use their belief in you as a bridge to reconnecting with your inspired life vision.

EVERYDAY INSPIRED:
CONSISTENT REGULAR ACTION ADDS UP

*I've noticed a new trend that I call "spiritual buli-
mia." People are eating, and then regurgitating all
sorts of inspiration, quotes, and advice, but have
no real power or evidence of success or change in
their own lives. They ingest all the self-help and inspirational materials, but they don't digest it. They
are taking it all in, but not actually implementing
the behaviors, changing the thoughts, and eliminating the patterns to have lives that should be the
by-product of such voracious consumption.*

—*Staci J. Shelton*

Self-help is a booming field, evidenced by the 164,361 titles
that appear on an amazon.com search in April 2011. But
simply because information is readily available does not
mean that you will magically get the benefits by reading,
understanding, and even teaching the concepts to others. In
order to strengthen any muscle, habit of thinking, or skill in
your life—*you must use it or you lose it*, as the old adage
goes. This is true for living an inspired life, just as it is true
for developing and maintaining strong abs and biceps.

For this reason you must consistently think the thoughts, feel the feelings, speak the words, and do the actions that reflect your desires. Jane Umanoff, psychotherapist and life coach, describes her consistent regular practice:

When I am living aligned in my inspired life vision I feel excited waking up in the morning. I nurture this excitement by starting my day with an inspirational reading with my husband as we have our morning coffee and watch the birds snacking at our bird feeders. This sets the tone for my day, keeps my connection with my husband alive, gives me a taste of the natural world, and feeds me spiritually. Then, throughout the day, I nourish my body with healthy food. I make sure to spend time in nature a few times each week. I practice yoga five times a week. It is a very big thing being physically fit, emotionally healthy, intellectually inspired, spiritually connected, having a creative project, and making time in my life for my children, grandchildren, and friends, in addition to my full-time psychotherapy and coaching practice!

When I don't do these things consistently, due to a busy schedule or unexpected challenges, my day will still be okay because I have had a practice focused on living an inspired life since 1990 but I have more of a flat feeling throughout the day. Since I want to feel inspired, happy, joyous, and grateful every day, I have to make a

conscious decision every morning to take the actions that
sustain these feelings. When I don't start the day taking
the actions that nourish inspiration in my life, I am not as
mindful during the day.

INSPIRED LIFE PRACTICE:
RECOMMIT TO YOURSELF EACH DAY

Make a list of actions you can take which can be part
of your inspired life daily practice. Your list may include:
meditation, yoga, reading a daily inspiration, spending
time in nature, exercise, prayer, journaling, and so on. On
your calendar, for each of the next thirty days, write down
at least one item from your list that you commit to doing.
You can repeat the items, or do a different one every day of
the week. Experiment and acknowledge yourself for your
actions. After the first thirty days, schedule inspired life
actions on your calendar for the next thirty days.

Remember: When you practice inspired life actions on
the days you are feeling good, inspired, and on-top-of-
the-world, you will then have greater access to them and
remember to do them sooner on the days when challenges
are present.

FIND A DAILY PRACTICE PARTNER

Invite a family member or friend to join you in a regular daily practice. If you live together, you might begin your morning with an inspirational reading and meditation. If you do not see one another daily, you may start your day with a phone call or video call, and each day one of you chooses the practice you will do that day. Create a structure that works for both of you. Having a buddy is a powerful resource in staying on track with a daily practice.

COMMITTED TO SERVICE—
MAKING A CONTRIBUTION

Service...
Giving what you don't have to give.
Giving when you don't need to give.
Giving because you want to give.

—Damien Hess

After the verb "to love," "to help" is the most
beautiful verb in the world.

—Bertha von Suttner

A cornerstone of living an inspired life is the generosity of spirit that is expressed in being of service and making a contribution. This is giving with no strings attached. This is giving with no scorekeeping. This is giving where you look beyond, *what's in it for me.* This is giving where both the giver and receiver are enriched through the experience—it may actually be unclear who is the giver and who is the receiver, in the eyes of the people involved. This is giving where your skills, talents, gifts, and abilities are given as an expression of your purpose and your desire to make a difference in the world—whether the world is represented by your family, your friends, your workplace, your community, or the larger global community.

Susyn's first assignment in graduate school was to "help someone." The powerful lessons she learned by completing this assignment continue to impact her life today. Here is Susyn's story:

On my first day of graduate school, my very first assignment was, help someone and write about it. I thought, "This will be easy, I like helping people." But it wasn't a matter of it being easy or hard, the assignment gave me an opportunity to explore how I defined being helpful and then hear what my classmates had learned as well.

It was clear that we all wanted to be helpful—we were enrolled in a graduate program in counseling! But prior to this assignment none of us had ever really looked at what being helpful meant to us. What I learned through that assignment has continued to influence my life and my work, now thirty-nine years later.

❀ *I learned that being helpful, being of service is not just about the doing; it is embodied in the attitude with which the help, the action, is offered. When help is offered and received with an openhearted attitude, there is a quality in the relationship formed between the giver and receiver that nourishes the human spirit.*

This connection can be felt whether the help is as simple as giving a pregnant woman a seat on a crowded subway or doing relief work in a place devastated by a natural disaster.

❀ *I learned that being of service is at its best when both the giver and the receiver know they are contributing to one another—not when one is the "have" and the other the "have not."*

❀ *I learned that people often have a difficult time receiving help, and yet, when you allow yourself to receive, you are offering the giver the opportunity to give and to make a contribution.*

❀ *I learned that in their heart of hearts, people want to make a difference. People want to make a contribution and when you remember on this planet we are One, then we can stop competing and open our hearts, treating one another as loving members of the same family—the human family.*

❀ *I learned that it is just as important to offer help, as it is to say "no" when you are*

stretched to your limit; and if you said "yes,"
just because you thought you should, you
would actually be dishonoring yourself.

❀ *I learned that often we desire to make a*
contribution, to be of service but we think
what we have to offer is of no real value or
we just don't know how. It doesn't occur to
us to ask the simple questions, "How may I
help? How may I serve?"

When living an inspired life you trust the promptings from within, to offer help and to practice random acts of kindness. As our dear friend Melinda Lee said, *"Living an inspired life is about making a difference on the planet. You're personally inspired by your life and your presence inspires others. Your energy is contagious. Your inspiration motivates others to take action. And you may never know the ripple effect that your act of kindness has in the world."*

Joan discovered that the most fulfilling success must include being of service to others. Here is Joan's story:

When I moved to Florida in 2002, I easily became a successful real estate agent. However, when the market collapsed in 2008, I could not in good conscience continue to be excited about just helping people buy homes. I was deeply aware of the impact of the devastated economy on Florida real estate and the pain and suffering many people were experiencing as their homes were now worth less than the mortgages they owed, and the possibility of fore-closure was becoming a reality for so many people.

Early one morning, I sat down to write in my journal exploring the question, "What do I want to do next?" A clear answer did not come, but another question did, "What do I love to do?" The answer popped into my mind, with rapid-fire speed, and I immediately, in bold letters, wrote in my journal, *I love to help people.*

I had a Master's Degree in Counseling and I thought, "Why not go back to my old profession—counseling and teaching." But the economy was in a downturn and the idea of landing a job as a counselor, after having been an entrepreneur since 1985, didn't seem like the most direct route to take.

I knew that to maintain my happiness and excitement about life, I needed to express my talents and strengths so I decided to volunteer my time and expertise at the Women's Resource Center in Sarasota, Florida. I offered vocational counseling on a volunteer basis. When the center needed a volunteer to lead their Empowerment and Self-Esteem Program, I jumped at the opportunity.

That was in 2008. I am still facilitating the groups. I have helped hundreds of women discover and connect with their inner strength and empower themselves to *change their lives. What a joy this has been. I know this is part of my God-given talent and when I express it, I am in sync with my purpose, my reason for being. This is a powerful feeling and it sustains and inspires me throughout the week.*

Using my talents and skills in ways that the women in the group blossom, as their self-esteem and self-confidence was ignited, made my heart sing. When your heart is singing, life unfolds and evolves in wonderful ways. I know that the service I offer, the contribution I am making through the Women's Resource Center, has played a vital role in Susyn and I being inspired to create www.self-esteem-experts.com, develop our Empowerment Program, The Mind Manual System, and even write this book!

When you help others you are helping yourself. I have said many times that the group members give me more than I give to them. I use this lesson in our group. Many of the participants are depressed because they have been out of work for months and years. When you are depressed, staying at home, waiting for the phone to ring to schedule a job interview, only feeds your depression. I encourage them to be of service to others, to express their talents and make a contribution to others. Some of the actions the women in the group have taken are: volunteering at the local animal shelter walking the dogs; singing in nursing homes; mentoring children in after-school programs; volunteering in the local library; teaching math in an inner city school; teaching computer skills to seniors; volunteering in their church; and the list goes on and on.

What has been amazing to the women who are contributing their time and talents is how being of service transforms how they feel about themselves, and in turn, they are more hopeful about their future while clearly positively impacting the lives of those they serve.

INSPIRED LIFE COMMITMENT:
MAKE A CONTRIBUTION, LARGE OR SMALL

Take on the assignment that Susyn was given on her first day of graduate school: Help someone, be of service, make a contribution, and write what you have learned about being helpful. Share your insights with three people.

Remember: Making a contribution is not about the magnitude of the act; it is about the desire to serve, to be of use, to share your gifts, talents, skills, and resources.

> An inspired life is a life in service, deeply connected to Source from within and co-creating a vision birthed from love, compassion and delight.
>
> —Myrissa Lai

OFFER YOUR TALENTS TO THOSE WHO NEED THEM

Make a list of your skills, talents, gifts, and abilities and a list of causes you believe in and want to support. Choose what you would like to offer and where you'd like to offer it; then take action to explore where and how you can best be of service.

PEOPLE POWER:
DISCOVERING YOUR COMMUNITY OF SUPPORT

It takes community to maintain a human.

—*Earon Davis*

Most of us, particularly those of us raised in Western cultures, have been programmed to value our ability to be independent. This point of view is reflected in the statement, "I can do it myself!" When a young child learns something new—to walk, to tie their shoes, particularly before Velcro took the place of many shoelaces—parents and loved ones can be heard applauding the mastering of this new skill and their child's greater independence.

There is no question that there is value in trusting our talents, skills, and abilities and to have access to our inner wisdom and follow that guidance as we find our way and set our course through life. Yet there is also a downside to an "I can do it myself" attitude. It leads to competition where you are successful if you are the winner and a failure if you are the loser. This need to always be in first place can be demoralizing for a person's self-esteem, self-confidence, and faith in themselves when they are not number one, and when the task at hand or the situation they are faced with is more than they are able to handle themselves.

This attitude can also prevent people from reaching out for support when they are in need. The belief *"I am a failure"* and not capable of navigating life's challenges is often experienced as shame and humiliation. In these dark times people have a tendency to isolate, to be consumed by self-abusive thoughts and addictions—losing hope in life itself, losing connection with the Greater Field of Life and conscious access to their creative potential to transform their experience. In the presence of these feelings, and the thoughts that generate them, living an inspired life does not appear to be a possibility.

Even for those of you who have not experienced the horrors of physical and emotional abuse in your life, you have still faced disappointment and loss whether it be the loss of a loved one, the loss of a job, a devastating medical diagnosis—and the list goes on. Finding yourself in a dark night of the soul, struggling with your faith, feeling alone in your misery is an experience all humans can relate to. For these reasons a community of support is an essential building block in consciously embodying and sustaining your vision for your inspired life.

Humans are social animals. It is through our relationships that we find support, both in sharing the joys of life as well as journeying through heart-wrenching experiences. While you are probably familiar with the words, "*Misery loves company*," it is in the midst of misery that courage is necessary to reach out for company, both seeking and allowing support.

> *At times our own light goes out and is rekindled by a spark from another person. Each of us has cause to think with deep gratitude of those who have lighted the flame within us.*
>
> —*Albert Schweitzer*

CONNECTING TO THE COLLECTIVE GOOD: CREATING A COMMUNITY OF SUPPORT

For some people their birth families are their source of support in times of need. Yet for many people it is in their families that they have felt most alone and misunderstood. So many of us seek support outside of our families. You can find a support group for every issue and problem people face—alcoholism, drug addiction, overeating, bipolar disorders, gambling, parents of children diagnosed with autism, divorce, etc. Name a category that represents a life challenge and there is a support group addressing that issue.

The power of group support has always been present, whether in the family group, tribal community, community church, or women gathering at the well, but it wasn't until 1935, when Alcoholics Anonymous began, that the power of a group of strangers sharing a common problem initiated the myriad of support groups available today.

We turn to a support group, to a community of support, when we feel alone and isolated, when we feel powerless in the face of our challenges. It is through this community of support that we ultimately reconnect with the Greater Field of Life that connects all people. We no longer feel alone and isolated when we are surrounded and encouraged by people who have journeyed through the misery we are feeling. We can use their belief in us, their stories of moving through obstacles and success as beacons that guide us to our personal north star.

I have come to know that "Misery loves company," doesn't mean you gather to complain, blame, and nourish a sense of victimization but, rather, when I know you have shared a similar experience then I no longer feel isolated, ashamed, and alone. It is through this connection with others that the door to possibility opens, the winding road of despair becomes straight, and the light at the end of the tunnel becomes visible.

Living an inspired life will not safeguard you from the challenges of life but being connected with a community of support will serve as the wind beneath your wings in the midst of these challenges. Whether your community is your family, your religious group, a group of close friends, or a formal support group, there are some commonalities they all share. A community of support:

❀ Acknowledges what you are feeling and provides a safe haven for you to express yourself.

❀ Is accepting and nonjudgmental of who you are and the situation you are in.

- ❀ Believes in you, your dreams, and your ability to evolve beyond the misery you are experiencing.

- ❀ Offers a shoulder to cry on when you break down and celebrates your breakthroughs.

- ❀ Offers feedback, suggestions, and advice when you ask for them.

- ❀ Nourishes you emotionally and spiritually.

- ❀ Focuses on moving forward and freeing your heart and mind from the wounds of the past.

- ❀ Sees your greatness.

Susyn has a long history of being involved with support groups, and she knows from firsthand experience what a lifeline they can be. Here is Susyn's story:

I have been involved in leading groups since I was in junior high school and worked with a Brownie Troop. In college and graduate school I formally learned about groups. While in graduate school I led a group for women who were preparing to live in a group home after having been institutionalized in a state mental hospital for between five to twenty-five years.

Since that time I have designed, facilitated, and led groups for:

   ❀   *People going through separation and divorce*

   ❀   *Parents of children born with severe physical and emotional disabilities*

   ❀   *Women in prison*

   ❀   *Assertiveness training*

   ❀   *Leadership development*

   ❀   *Building self-esteem and confidence*

   ❀   *Family members of people who had strokes*

   ❀   *Women in the midst of treatment for breast cancer*

   ❀   *Clients desiring loving relationships*

In all of these groups, whether they were very structured with a specific lesson plan or were focused on sharing what was going on right now for the participants, the feedback was always the same, "What's most helpful about this group is that I found out that I am not alone."

I knew this was true from personal experiences I had had and recently I have been reminded of this again—not from being a facilitator but from being a participant. In January 2010, I made a commitment to be in a new love relationship in my life. I was missing the intimacy, companionship and the opportunity to deepen and expand my capacity to give and receive love that can only occur inside of an intimate relationship—as friends, lovers, and companions. But this was an area of my life that had been challenging for me. I had been married twice and while I had many wonderful memories, I had serious doubts about whether the relationship of my dreams was a possibility. This may sound strange since I am a teacher of possibility and have been a cheerleader for the dreams of tens of thousands of people!

I knew I needed help. So I made the commitment to being in a new relationship a priority in my life. And the next thing I knew, I received an email describing a teleclass offered by Katherine Woodward Thomas, author of Calling in "The One," and Claire Zammit. I participated in the introductory teleclass and immediately signed up for the course, along with 799 other people.

The focus was on setting a clear intention for unprecedented love in our lives and transforming our personal internal obstacles to our vision of love fulfilled. The information on the calls was fantastic (so much so that I am now a Certified Calling in "The One" Coach!), the work was deep and powerful, and the support was and continues to be inspiring.

I was part of a small group in our online community. We had weekly reflection questions to respond to and we were instructed to give encouragement to at least three people in our group each week. This encouragement gave me the courage to dream big, to take risks, and to express the shame I had felt in being "unsuccessful" in relationships since I had been divorced twice. The support I received allowed me to upgrade my personal love identity and begin to believe that the relationship of my dreams is possible for me.

Needless to say, I am a cheerleader for support groups!

INSPIRED LIFE ACTION:

CREATING A NETWORK OF SUPPORT HELPS ALL INVOLVED! Identify an area of your life where you need support—health, relationships, career, finances—and connect with others for support. You may actually participate in a formal support group or join with friends who are committed to the same vision and use one another as your vision keepers. (See "How to Create a Support Group" in the appendix.)

Remember: Reaching out for support in time of need is a reflection of your courage, not of failure. Sustaining an inspired life requires a community of support.

CELEBRATING THE PEOPLE IN YOUR LIFE

An inspired life is a life lived with great curiosity and compassion. It is a life lived at the edge of vulnerability so that giving and receiving are its driving forces. It is a life which at the end radiates kindness and wisdom, dignity, and grace.

—Michael Colberg

Another form of support is taking the time to celebrate the people in your life. Everyone wants to be loved and recognized. When love and recognition are given with an open heart our spirits soar and we offer people the opportunity to see themselves through the eyes of those who love and care for them.

Too often, while we may be thinking loving thoughts of others, we fail to express them directly. As a reflection of the inspired life you desire, actively expressing your love is a priceless gift you can give over and over and over again.

Joan's family and friends celebrated and honored her on her fiftieth birthday in a way that changed her life. Here is Joan's story:

As my fiftieth birthday approached, I felt I had it all—a loving husband, a successful business I had just sold, and a cadre of wonderful friends who had helped and supported me through my life, personally and professionally. I decided to host a retirement/birthday party and invite my friends to celebrate with me in Jamaica.

Susyn, we'd been friends for twenty years by this time, wanted to make this birthday very special for me, and give me the best present in the world. She decided to make a book for me, with personal tributes and messages from everyone who came to the party.

The night of my big birthday party, as we sat eating birthday cake, Susyn stood up and said, "I have a gift for you, that we all contributed to, so you can see who you are through the eyes of the people who love you," and she gave me the book, "In Celebration of Joan's 50th Birthday."

Feeling too embarrassed to read the messages in front of my family and friends during my party, I got up early the next morning and sat down, alone, to read it. My heart filled to overflowing with love as I got to see, in written form, what every human being wants most: love, recognition, and appreciation. Wow! This was a powerful gift. Through the words I read, I saw the impact I had on other people. I did get to see who I am through the eyes of the people who love me. Receiving this gift and allowing the words to touch my heart was a powerful, positive, and life-renewing experience.

At that moment I had a vision: "Everyone in the world should have a book like this. It makes people feel special." Celebrateahero.com was born—a website where you can pay tribute and create a group memory book for the people you love. Celebrate is going into its twelfth year of operation. Thousands of people have been celebrated. Celebrate continues to bring happiness and joy to people who give the book and to people who receive their book. I love what it does and I consider it one of my greatest achievements because the power of giving and receiving love is what makes the world a special place.

I still find it quite amazing: my dear friend followed her impulse, her desire to give me the best gift in the world. She asked others to participate and express their love for me. My heart was filled with love and appreciation and now, twelve years later, this gift keeps on giving.

(Note: Since 2003, celebrateahero.com gift books have been made available, free of charge, to celebrate military personnel actively serving in harm's way, in places like Iraq and Afghanistan.)

INSPIRED LIFE PRACTICE:

RECOGNIZE AND CELEBRATE YOUR COMMUNITY

Express your love and appreciation to the people in your life. Make a celebrateahero.com book, send an email, write a letter, make a phone call, make a video card. Don't wait for a special occasion—make today a special occasion and celebrate the people you love.

Remember: Your words of love and appreciation are a priceless gift. Share this gift and notice how your capacity to give and receive love expands.

NOW IS YOUR TIME

An inspired life is remembering that we are Star-born and Earthbound.

—*Reverend Lorraine Simone*

Congratulations, you are clearly on the path to living your inspired life vision. You now have the information and the practices to illuminate your inspired life path and feast on the infinite possibility that life offers.

As a final reminder, remember:

❀ You are a co-creative partner with the Greater Field of Life; your work is to embody your vision of your inspired life through your thoughts, beliefs, feelings, words, choices, and actions.

❀ Thought charged with energy, spoken of with authority, and acted on with conviction, is the foundation of your experience.

❀ Your greatest point of power is the present moment, step into it consciously and with love.

❀ Breakdowns are the doorway to breakthroughs.

An inspired life is one in which you are fully present in each moment and allow yourself to be informed by the presence of that moment.
—Gaelyn Larrick

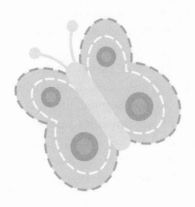

AFTERWARD—THE JOURNEY CONTINUES

It is easy to think that the biggest challenge in writing a book is sitting down and doing the actual writing. But since I am most motivated in the face of a deadline, when I finally sit down to write, the words generally flow effortlessly through my fingertips.

My biggest challenge in writing this book has been that I lived every chapter anew; because while I know words are powerful, I also know the energy generating the words is what creates the connection between the author and the reader.

So while I have known for many years, decades in fact, much of the information in this book, I also know that living my commitment to my inspired life vision continually challenges me with opportunities to expand and deepen my capacity for allowing joy. And it is breakdowns that have offered me the chance to break through old patterns and to continually embody my ever-evolving inspired life vision.

Just when I thought I had finished this manuscript, I blindly fell into what felt like a bottomless pit. I share this story with you now so that you will understand that bumps, potholes and detours in the road do appear, they can take us by surprise. Just as with our in-breath and out-breath, in life we experience expansion and contraction. By using the information and tools which fill this book my inspired life path was illuminated and I had access to my ladder and road map so it wasn't necessary for me to be consumed by fear, judgments, worry, anger, and hopelessness for very long. I lived this experience in twenty-two hours:

I had applied to be a master coach in a program I was more than qualified for. While I knew that there were more applicants than openings, I felt confident that I would be chosen. The applications were to be submitted on a Friday and the first coaches' meeting was scheduled for the following Monday.

I woke up Monday morning and while meditating I became anxious as I thought, "What if I haven't been chosen?" As I wrote about this in my journal I began to feel ashamed. I had decided as a child that I'd be the smart child in my family, and what if, now, that wasn't being recognized, what did this mean about me and who I am if not the smart one?

I couldn't seem to shake this empty feeling in the pit of my stomach. I decided to get some information. I emailed the office, not expecting to hear from them immediately since I'm on the East Coast and they're in California. I emailed my coaching colleagues, who I knew had also applied for these coaching positions. Within fifteen minutes

I found out that two of my colleagues had been accepted and they had heard of their acceptance on Saturday.

I felt as though a lightning bolt sword had pierced right through my heart. I wrote this in an email to one of my vision keepers and felt her support immediately but it didn't ease my sadness, anger, and shame. Then I got the official email—I had not been chosen.

My tears flowed and continued as I learned that the other three members of my support pod had all been accepted. Then an onslaught of judgments began to thunderously fill my mind: "I'm smarter than her, I have more experience than her, I was coaching him...blah, blah, blah."

Fifteen minutes later one of my closest friends arrived for one of her rare lunch visits. She said "hello," gave me a hug and before I could say a word my tears were dripping onto the floor; floodgates had opened.

I told her that I hadn't been chosen and recited my long list of why I was a better choice than some of the people who were chosen. Somewhere in this litany of my self-importance the words, "I wasn't chosen" stopped me in my tracks. This thought generated very old feelings of not being chosen by boys, by groups I wanted to be part of, and now, feeling that I hadn't been chosen because I wasn't smart enough had me feeling devastated.

I shared all these thoughts and feelings with Eve and after we exhausted that conversation she said, "Oh, I've been meaning to tell you that the man I have wanted to introduce you to, took a look at your website and he emailed me to tell me that he wouldn't be calling you because he thinks you're too accomplished for him." I immediately started laughing, a deep, deep belly laugh. There I was feeling as though I wasn't smart enough to be accepted for this coaching project and here was a man who didn't want to meet me because he thought I was too smart, so he didn't choose me!

In that moment it became crystal clear that this wasn't about the coaching project; this was about my long held, deeply felt belief that I Am Not Chosen.

Eve left and within fifteen minutes my dear friend Mary Angela was at my door. We are angels in one another's lives and make time to be with one another every week—her timing this week was impeccable! I shared with her what I was feeling, we both cried as our deep wounds generated by our beliefs of not being chosen surfaced. By the time she left I felt embraced, drained and still had lingering judgments about the other coaches moving in and out of my mind and the money I wouldn't be making.

I went to the gym, I watched a movie, and had a restless night's sleep. When I got out of bed in the morning I was still aware of my judgments about the other coaches stumbling around in my thoughts. As I walked into the living room, headed for my meditation chair, I was stopped in my tracks, as I thought, "A lightning bolt did go through my heart yesterday. It opened my heart." And with that thought, all of the judgments were silenced and I felt a surge of energy move through me. I felt whole, inspired, bursting with love.

As I sat down to meditate I saw the previous twenty-two hours unfold before my eyes: I had immediately been met with support from my pod; two of my closest friends just happened to be coming to my house for a visit; I didn't have any appointments so I could be with me; and I used the tools from my inspired life tool box.

It is now four weeks later and I have been evolving my patterns of the past in terms of embracing the younger parts of me who for so very long I hadn't chosen. So the journey continues, as I am empowered to allow all of me to shine as I declare my inspired life vision: I am a Student of Love—I Am a Teacher of Love—I Am Love!

Susyn Reeve
Hampton Bays, NY

APPENDIX

CONTRIBUTORS' WEBSITES

Lyndra Hearn Antonson www.loverelationshipcoach.com
Mary Angela Buffo www.anandayogawellness.com
Diana Daffner www.intimacyretreats.com
Jody Florman www.jflormanartgallery.com
Katie Freiling www.katiefreiling.com
Robert Fritz www.robertfritz.com
Gail Lynne Goodwin www.inspiremetoday.com
Lee McCormick www.spiritrecovery.com
   and www.recoveryranch.com
David Riklan www.selfgrowth.com
Sheri Rosenthal www.journeysofthespirit.com
   and www.withforgiveness.com
Peter Russell www.peterrussell.com
Remez Sasson www.successconsciousness.com
Staci J. Shelton www.stacijshelton.com
Rev. Lorraine Simone www.moonfiremeetinghouse.com
Katherine Woodward Thomas and Claire Zammit
   www.callingintheone.com
   and www.femininepower.com

BOOKS THAT HAVE INSPIRED US

The Four Agreements by don Miguel Ruiz
The Mastery of Love by don Miguel Ruiz
Living Life as a Thank You by Nina Lesowitz and Mary
    Beth Sammons
The Biology of Belief by Bruce Lipton
The Path of Least Resistance by Robert Fritz
Calling in "The One" by Katherine Woodward Thomas
Choose Peace and Happiness by Susyn Reeve
Banish Mind Spam by Sheri Rosenthal
Seth Speaks by Jane Roberts
The Road Less Traveled by M. Scott Peck
A Course in Miracles by Foundation for Inner Peace
One Day My Soul Just Opened Up by Iyanla Vanzant
Prayer: Does It Make Any Difference? by Philip Yancey
Entering the Castle by Caroline Myss
Spiritual Economics by Eric Butterworth
Change Your Thoughts, Change Your Life by Wayne Dyer
Living With Joy by Sanaya Roman
Ask and It Is Given by Esther and Jerry Hicks
WITH Forgiveness ~ Are You Ready? Personal E-Work-
    book by Susyn Reeve and Sheri Rosenthal
Women, Food, and God by Geneen Roth

A Course in Weight Loss by Marianne Williamson
The Map by Colette Baron-Reid
Writing Down Your Soul by Janet Conner

FORMING AN INSPIRED LIFE CIRCLE

While the information in this book is life transforming, our personal experience along with the feedback from our clients, indicates that implementing it in your everyday lives requires dedicated effort.

We have also found that having a support group consisting of a circle of individuals actively committed to living an inspired life can significantly accelerate your ability to live your inspired life vision. These groups are self-sustaining, governed by group consensus, with facilitation rotated among members. When you join an inspired life circle, you are joining a network of committed individuals dedicated to consciously living life filled with love, peace, abundance, and happiness!

What do you do during a typical inspired life circle? Meetings begin and end with a prayer, music, or a reading chosen by the facilitator. You may choose to focus on a specific chapter of the book, have a discussion of the lesson, and also share your challenges, experiences, and ideas related to that chapter. You might even invite a guest speaker to join you. While we suggest working through the book chapter-by-chapter, it is ultimately up to your circle to develop a format that is most supportive of your members' personal expressions and desires.

How do I start an inspired life circle? By setting your intent, you begin the process of creating an inspired life circle.

How do I find members for my inspired life circle? Start by sharing your desire to start a circle with friends and family. Place a post on Facebook and a tweet on Twitter. You can also post flyers in your local grocery store, library, coffee shop, New Thought church, bookstore, or place an ad in your local paper. Once you start spreading the word and stay focused on your inspired life circle vision people are sure to come!

Creating a Sacred Space begins with your intention and is then supported by the environment you create. While it is not necessary to do anything special, you may want to use candles, special objects, pictures, flowers, music, to remind you that you are entering a sacred space which is connected to a larger purpose and dream of heaven on earth. All circle members contribute to the sacred space by their presence and their commitment to honoring the divine in each other.

All that is needed for the physical meeting space is a clean, quiet, safe environment. It does not matter if your circle gathers on the floor of your living room, in a community center, or even in a rented space. What is important is that you gather with conscious intent, respect, and integrity.

The Role of the Facilitator: Select a facilitator prior to the close of each circle gathering. Rotating this responsibility among circle members is ideal so that each member has the opportunity to be a leader as well as a participant. The facilitator's role is to:

❀ Identify the topic for the meeting, preferably at the previous meeting. You may follow the chapters of the book from the beginning to the end, or based on the agreement of the group members, the facilitator may choose the topic. The decision of how to choose the topic for each meeting will be agreed upon at your first gathering. Remember to be flexible since a specific topic may generate emotional reactions and the group may want to continue with a particular topic until they feel complete.

❀ Keep time so each meeting begins and ends promptly. We recommend meetings be at least ninety minutes, to ensure the participation of each member and an opportunity for an in-depth exploration of the lesson.

❀ Maintain the circle guidelines. Should a member forget a guideline, the facilitator will reinforce it.

❀ Maintain the basic circle format. This format is designed to support the intention of living an inspired life.

❀ Lead the opening and closing prayer, or choose a reading or song to mark the opening and closing of the sacred circle.

INSPIRED LIFE CIRCLE GUIDELINES

With the publication of *The Millionth Circle* by Jean Shinoda Bolen, in 1999, circles have formed and gathered throughout the world to support people in giving voice to their deepest desires, and, in the words of Gandhi, *"to be the change they wish to see in the world."* The following guidelines have been used worldwide and we suggest you follow them in your circle:

❀ Consider your circle a sacred space. Agree upon what is to be held in confidence. For instance, the agreement *"What is spoken in the circle, stays in the circle,"* helps to ensure a safe environment for sharing experiences and feelings.

❀ Begin and end with a prayer, song, or inspirational reading.

❀ Open and close the circle by hearing each member's voice. (This can be as simple as stating your name, a word or two to describe how you are feeling right now, a question you would like answered, or what you have learned during the gathering.)

❀ Only one person speaks at a time. There is no cross talk. You may use a talking stick or power object, which is held by the person speaking. When the speaker is finished, the talking stick is passed to the next speaker. This can be done in a clockwise fashion, and if a person chooses not to speak, s/he says, "pass" and gives the talking stick to the next person. Or the talking stick can simply be passed from one speaker to the next based on who is moved to speak. Everyone is encouraged to add their voices to the circle.

❀ Refrain from gossiping about people outside of your circle, as well as with members of the circle about one another. Gossip contains judgment and is clearly at odds with acceptance.

❀   Allow several moments of silence between speakers, to acknowledge each speaker has been heard. Speak and then silence, speak and then silence.

❀   Speak and listen from the heart. This includes listening without an agenda, suspending judgment, being curious, and listening for the underlying meaning, "the music behind the words." Practice listening for wisdom as it comes through each participant.

❀   Encourage and welcome diverse points of view. It is not about making folks right or wrong—allow yourself and everyone else their own point of view. The idea is to ultimately transcend all points of view, and the circle is a wonderful place to put those teachings into practice. There is no need to change anyone or anything. Break the habit of "piggy-backing," when you formulate your answer based on the statement said before, and modifying it to make yourself "right."

❀   Give the speaker your full attention without formulating what you will say. This means not answering a question until the person has completely finished what they have to say and allowing a moment of silence.

❀   Share leadership and resources.

❀   Decide together how decisions will be made. It is desirable to work toward consensus when possible. Some common decisions to be agreed upon are: the length of the meeting, the meeting format, who will lead the meeting, the location, whether or not to collect donations and how donations will be used, what is expected of participants regarding attendance and participation, and the circle guidelines to follow.

❀   Offer experience instead of advice. Share your experience and feelings in the circle, not your advice about how someone else "should" see something or act in a particular situation. If someone requests to hear another point of view you may offer it. A more supportive method of assisting someone in detaching from a difficult point of view is to ask a question like, "Is it possible to consider seeing this situation from another point of view?" or "Is that way of seeing things coming from love or fear?" or "Is your belief supporting your inspired life vision?"

❀ When in doubt, pause, and silently ask for guidance. This includes listening to your inner guidance before speaking. Request silence and reflection in the circle when you feel it is needed.

❀ Stay focused in the present, rather than story-telling about the past. If you have current feelings about a past experience, focus on your feelings rather than reporting a "there and then" history.

INSPIRED LIFE CIRCLE FORMAT

❀ The facilitator opens each meeting by asking members to observe a moment of silence and then leading a centering meditation. Taking a moment of silence and connecting to the present moment through your breath sets the intent and creates a sacred space. This is a time when you may light a candle to shine the light on your inspired life vision and your intention for your circle.

❀ Circle members recite a prayer (you may use "The Prayer for Peace and Happiness"), listen to a song, and/or the facilitator reads words of inspiration chosen by the facilitator or the group.

THE PRAYER FOR PEACE AND HAPPINESS

Today with heartfelt gratitude I live my life through the experience of peace and happiness. I easily focus my attention on thoughts that enhance the flow of love in my life. I know that I create my experience through the point of view I choose. Through inviting and allowing peace and happiness, I acknowledge that I am peace, I am happiness, I am love. I ask for and receive all the help available to me, visible and invisible, to easily release habit patterns of fear, to have faith in a loving future, and to live as love in the present.

To the eternal peace and happiness of all—and so it is.

—Susyn Reeve

❀ Set the intention—the facilitator or a member of the group reads the inspired life circle intention and the circle guidelines to ensure that this intention is in the conscious awareness of your circle members. We encourage you to make copies of your intention to give to your circle members. You can use the following intention or create one of your own:

We're grateful you've joined us in our commitment to live our inspired life visions. Together, we will:

❀ *Transform the fear-based beliefs and judgments within us that cause human conflict, pain, and suffering.*

❀ *Adopt specific practices to help us evolve patterns of the past.*

❀ *Practice clear techniques and actions necessary to live an inspired life.*

❀ *Create a community supporting an inspired life for all members.*

❀ The facilitator begins the check-in process to add each person's voice to the sacred circle.

❀ The facilitator begins the "body" of the meeting, which was decided at the end of the previous meeting. This may be a discussion of a particular chapter, practice of a particular exercise, or the introduction of a guest speaker. The facilitator can prepare for this by having a question ready to pose to the circle or an exercise prepared.

❀ If your circle has agreed to collect donations, you can pass a basket at the end of the "body" of your meeting or you can have a basket in a visible and convenient location. The facilitator will remind circle members to give a donation with love and how the circle's donations are being used.

❀ The facilitator for the next meeting will be identified and s/he will state the topic for the next meeting. For the next meeting you may choose to follow the chapters of the book or the circle may choose to further explore what was discussed in this meeting.

✿ The facilitator begins the check-out process to add each person's voice to the closing of the sacred circle.

- A closing prayer or reading is offered by the facilitator or a designated member of the group.

- The facilitator closes the circle with a moment of silence to center and ground each participant as they connect with their breath and honor their inspired life vision.

- If a candle has been lit, the facilitator extinguishes the light and the circle gathering is officially closed.

ABOUT THE AUTHORS

 SUSYN REEVE, M.ED., as a teenager, wrote in her journal, "What would the world be like if everyone loved themselves?" This question has guided her fierce commitment to partnering with clients to expand their capacity to give and receive love, by removing their inner obstacles to love and living the life they desire. She has done this in many roles over her thirty-five years of experience as a transformational coach, educator, corporate consultant, and interfaith minister. She is the award-winning author of *Choose Peace and Happiness*, co-creator of www.self-esteem-experts.com, and a Certified Calling in "The One" Coach. Susyn lives on the east end of Long Island, NY. Photo by Demetriad Studios.

 JOAN BREINER, M.ED., is Vice President of the National Association for Self-Esteem. Joan has a Master's Degree in Counseling and Education and has taught at New York University. She is a successful businesswoman. Her businesses have been featured in print, and on radio and television. Most recently, she is the empowerment group leader at the Women's Resource Center in Sarasota, FL. She has also cofounded www.self-esteem-experts.com, www.celebrateahero.com, and The Mind Manual System. Joan is passionate about helping people understand how to open their minds and hearts to the creative potential of who they are. Joan lives in Sarasota, FL. Photo by Karen Wantuck.

PERMISSIONS

TO OUR READERS

Viva Editions publishes books that inform, enlighten, and entertain. We do our best to bring you, the reader, quality books that celebrate life, inspire the mind, revive the spirit, and enhance lives all around. Our authors are practical visionaries: people who offer deep wisdom in a hopeful and helpful manner. Viva was launched with an attitude of growth and we want to spread our joy and offer our support and advice where we can to help you live the Viva way: vivaciously!

We're grateful for all our readers and want to keep bringing you books for inspired living. We invite you to write to us with your comments and suggestions, and what you'd like to see more of. You can also sign up for our online newsletter to learn about new titles, author events, and special offers.

Viva Editions
2246 Sixth St.
Berkeley, CA 94710
www.vivaeditions.com
(800) 780-2279
Follow us on Twitter @vivaeditions
Friend/fan us on Facebook